READING AND PRAYING
THE NEW TESTAMENT

Reading and Praying
the New Testament
A Book-by-Book Guide for Catholics

Peter Kreeft

CHARIS

Servant Publications
Ann Arbor, Michigan

The chapters in this book first appeared in article form in issues of the
National Catholic Register during the years of 1990 and 1991.

Published by Servant Publications
P.O. Box 8617
Ann Arbor, Michigan 48107

Cover design by Kelly Nelson.

     95 10 9 8 7 6 5 4

Printed in the United States of America

ISBN 0-89283-755-1

Library of Congress Cataloging-in-Publication Data

Kreeft, Peter.
   Reading and praying the New Testament : a book-by-book
guide for Catholics / Peter Kreeft.
     p. cm.
  ISBN 0-89283-755-1
  1. Bible. N.T.—Criticism, interpretation, etc. I. Title.
BS2361.2.K74   1992
225.6'1—dc20   92-7557

Contents

Introduction

Of making of many books there is no end, and much study is a weariness of the flesh.   **Eccl 12:12**

THIS SCRIPTURE IS ESPECIALLY TRUE of books about the Book: there are many of them, and most are terribly wearisome. Why another one on the New Testament? Why this book?

First, it is for beginners, especially Catholics. People simply do not read as much or as well today as they used to. They especially do not read or know the Bible nearly as well as they used to. There are more beginners today, both Protestants and Catholics. Ironically, in the past even Catholics knew the Bible better than they do today, even though Vatican II strongly called for a renewal of Scripture reading among Catholics. A book like this would probably have been superficial and superfluous fifty years ago. Today we desperately need to go back to the Bible basics.

Second, this book is short and simple. Each chapter can be read over a cup of coffee and a muffin. It is not theological scholarship. I am not a professional Bible scholar, just an amateur, a lover of God.

Third, this book is meant to be practical, something to use, something more like a lab manual than a textbook. I hope it sends you to the Bible for reading and prayer. Reading and praying the Bible, especially the New Testament, is not the same as reading and praying with another book. I think we should read the Bible prayerfully and pray

7

biblically. Since this is God's Word, reading *and* praying it should be part of the same fundamental process. To put it another way, Bible reading is not just something to be added to prayer; rather, it is (or should ideally be) a form of prayer, if it is consciously read in the presence of God.

It may sound strange to so unify these two things, prayer and Bible reading, that you can *pray the Bible.* How can you *pray* a *book?* But (1) the Bible is not just a book, it is God's personal love letter to your soul. And (2) biblical prayer is not just your mind praying, it is God's mind praying, God's book praying, through you.

This book is unlike any other book. It's alive. It's "the sword of the Spirit" (Eph 6:17). It cuts your very being apart (Heb 4:12). It's a seed that springs to life (Lk 8), dry bones that come to life (Ez 37). It is an extremely dangerous book: dangerous to your sin, sloth, selfishness, and self-satisfaction. It should carry warning labels to spiritual sleepers who hate alarm clocks.

Praying the Bible is also unlike any other kind of prayer, because other prayer is from us to God, while this is *from God* through us back to God. In praying the Bible we align ourselves with God's very mind and will. The very act of praying the Bible is a fulfillment of the prayer, "Thy will be done," which is the most basic and essential key to achieving our whole purpose on earth, holiness and happiness.

In Catholic theology, Scripture is the primary "sacramental." A sacramental, like a sacrament, is a sign that is an occasion of grace. But it does not give grace by itself, *ex opere operato*, as the sacraments do. It depends on how we use it. But like the sacraments, the Bible is "a visible sign instituted by Christ to give grace," and it "effects what it signifies"—the two classic definitions of sacraments.

Think through every word in those two definitions for a minute, and you will see the sacramental power of this book. But remember, that power comes wholly from two free wills: God's and yours. The book is only the Spirit's sword. You must give it an opening by exposing your mind and heart and will to its cutting edge.

It is especially appropriate to speak of reading and praying the New Testament. The New Testament presents Christ. It is a sign pointing to Christ and his kingdom, his reign in our souls and minds and hearts. But it not only *signifies* this, it *effects* it when we read and pray it like no other book. It becomes a means of grace, a conduit of the kingdom coming to earth—that little but important bit of earth that is your mind and will. Then it transforms your life (which your mind and will control), and then bits of your world (which your life influences).

It "gives grace." How do you get grace? The same way you get wet. You don't do it yourself, God does it. But you have to go where God is, just as you have to go outside in the rain to get wet. Reading and praying the New Testament is putting yourself in the way, standing in God's great waterfall of "living water." If you stand in the street, you'll get hit by a truck. If you stand in the New Testament, you'll get kissed by God. It is God's mistletoe.

The Bible is also God's bread for our souls, especially the New Testament. Christ is our meat. One place you find meat is in sandwiches. Christ is like the meat in the sandwich of God's Word. A steady diet of the entire Bible is guaranteed to put spiritual muscle onto you.

In using this book as a guide to reading and praying the New Testament, don't make the mistake of only reading this book and not the New Testament itself. Instead, read one or two of my chapters and then read and pray the relevant book or books in the New Testament.

I recommend that you read a section or chapter from the particular book in the New Testament each day. Read at the pace that is right for you. Read prayerfully and reflectively. Led by the Holy Spirit, close your time of reading and prayer by reflecting on a key verse or two. Ask God to show you how these verses apply to your life. You may want to use some of the verses that I have highlighted in my book during your times of scriptural prayer and reflection.

The most important practical point I can possibly make about reading the New Testament is the very same as the most practical point I can possibly make about praying. *How* you do it, *when* you do it, even *where* you do it are all important, but by far the most important thing is to *do* it! Here are infinite treasure troves, endlessly fertile fields, forever fecund gardens, inexhaustibly mysterious woods, limitless ocean depths, wild and wonderful waves to surf with your spirit. (Yes, reading the New Testament prayerfully is like spiritual surfing!) Read. Pray. Do. Enjoy. Chew. Digest. Grow.

ONE

The Good News of Jesus Christ: Introduction to the Gospels

A NY *ONE* OF THE FOUR GOSPELS is inexhaustible. Libraries of books have been written about them and saints and scholars alike have devoted lifetimes to reading, praying, and studying them. Even if the whole human race meditated on one of the Gospels for a thousand years, they could not exhaust its riches.

The word "gospel" is a modernization of the Old English "gospell" (or "God-spell"), meaning "good news." The original Greek word is *eu-angellos* (Latin, *evangelium*), meaning "good-message." The words "angel" (messenger) and "evangelism" (preaching this news) come from *eu-angellos.*

Two unique facts about Christianity emerge from this word.

First, Christianity is *news:* concrete facts, specific miraculous events that really happened and were seen in this space-time world of ours. All other religions (except Judaism) are essentially abstract truths, philosophies, moralities, laws, mysticisms, techniques, psychologies, rituals, or social systems—something abstract and timeless.

Second, it's *good* news. J.R.R. Tolkien says, "There is no tale ever told that men more wish were true." Rightly understood,

stood, it is "tidings of great joy." But in the modern world it's often *not* rightly understood, and is seen as *bad* news: as repressive, pessimistic, negative, dehumanizing, and threatening. That fact says nothing about Christianity, but a lot about the modern mind.

The "Gospel" does not mean first of all the four *books* we know as the Gospels, but the news they report, real events in which God's plan of salvation is revealed. The "Gospel" was preached, believed, and lived for years before these books were written. This simple fact refutes the claim that Christianity *essentially* rests on the Bible. Our unbroken link to Christ is indeed the Gospel (that is, the good news about Christ); but the written Gospels make clear that this unbroken link was first forged in the living Church, shaped in its prayer life, meditation, good works, and apostolic preaching *prior* to any of the written texts we now possess. The Gospels are four of the books the Church—our divinely appointed teacher—wrote and uses to teach us. We must never separate our textbook from our teacher.

The Gospels are placed in the order we have them because tradition has always claimed they were composed in that order. Many modern scholars think *Mark* came first, *Matthew* using most of *Mark* and adding to it. But a controversial and important recent book claims that there is strong evidence that *Matthew* was written first, and in Hebrew. The grammatical idioms and the word structures and word play in *Matthew* make much more sense if they were translations into Greek of a Hebrew original.

What is the significance of the fact that there are four Gospels? First, it fulfills the prophecy in *Ezekiel* 1. The Church has always interpreted the four "living creatures" full of eyes in Ezekiel's vision as symbolic of the angels of the four evangelists. They also reappear in *Revelation* 4.

Second, the number four symbolizes completeness or universality in ancient thought. For example, "the four winds" blow over the whole earth. These four Gospels were written to all four possible audiences in the ancient world, thus encompassing the whole world. *Matthew* was written mainly for Jews, *Mark* for Romans, *Luke* for Greeks, and *John* for everyone. The same point of Christ's universality was symbolized by the sign on the cross: the charge against Jesus was written in Hebrew, Latin, and Greek, thus showing the whole world's guilt and the whole world's salvation.

Third, the fact that there are four accounts and not just one means that we can do cross-checking, like triangulation. This makes a very strong case for the historical reliability of the story. If the Gospels did not contain miraculous events, historians would accept them as accurate and factual just as they accept ancient secular documents. Indeed, the Gospels are in better shape than any other ancient record: we have more copies and earlier copies of them than of any other ancient record.

But aren't there contradictions among them?

No substantive ones. The minor discrepancies they contain are exactly what you would expect from four independent, honest eyewitnesses to any events. If they told *exactly* the same story, we would suspect copying and collusion.

What are the minor discrepancies?

1. Some concern numbers. For example, were there two angels at Christ's tomb (*Luke*) or one (*Matthew* and *Mark*)? The Bible is more concerned with quality than quantity.

2. The order of events is often inverted. Only *Luke* claims to be an orderly account (Lk 1:3). Luke could have meant three things "chronological, logical or spatial sequence." Given the parallel to Acts 11:4 and the dominant theme of promise and fulfillment of God's action in Christ (*Luke's Gospel*) and the Church (*Acts of the Apostles*), you could say that Luke's fundamental principle of organization is "[theo]logical sequence" which follows the "chronological sequence" of his sources, which he read very carefully and used with great skill.

3. Events are sometimes compressed. For example, sayings Jesus uttered on various occasions in the other Gospels are put in a single sermon in *Matthew* (the "Sermon on the Mount," Mt 5-7).

4. Quotations are not always word for word. Parallel passages in different Gospels usually differ slightly, but the substance is always the same.

5. The borderline between where Christ's words end and the evangelist's interpretation of them begins is not always clear, especially in *John* (for example, see Jn 3), since the ancients used no quotation marks.

Thus fundamentalists have a hard time justifying the infallibility of every detail. Yet the Gospels hold up very well when scrutinized by a modern, scientific, open-mindedly skeptical historical-textual investigator (as distinct from some Scripture scholars with pet theories to defend).

One such skeptical investigator, Frank Morrison, tried to disprove Christ's resurrection by a scientific, historical study of the texts, and ended up converting. Morrison concluded that the only explanation for all the data is a real resurrection. His book, *Who Moved the Stone?*, written in the 1920s, is still in print.

All four Gospels share common features in their structure:

- They center totally on Christ, especially on his person and work.
- They present his person as both human (Son of Man) and divine (Son of God).
- They present his work as both words (teachings) and deeds (miracles).
- They present his most important work as dying and rising from the dead.
- They present him as "Jesus," that is, the Savior from sin.
- They show both his power and his love.
- They begin no later than John the Baptist and end no earlier than the resurrection.

- They are written by eyewitnesses (Matthew, John) or those who interviewed eyewitnesses (Mark, Luke). Although this is disputed, nearly all Scripture scholars would concede that all the Gospels are based on reliable eyewitness accounts, regardless of who actually wrote and compiled them. My personal view is the former since each of the evangelists claims ownership, and each is supported by longstanding tradition and, in some cases, textual evidence in the Gospels themselves. For example, in the case of John, whose authorship is usually questioned the most, see John 21:24-25 and consider it in light of the preceding verses 20-23. As the Beloved Disciple, John is clearly claiming authorship here. Further, all the early Church Fathers ascribe the fourth Gospel to John.

The Gospels can be used in at least three different ways. First, they are the data for enquiring skeptics, providing historical evidence for the faith.

Second, they are the primary devotional, meditational reading to deepen our faith as Christians. They are the place where we meet Christ. St. Teresa of Avila said she never found anything as powerful as the Gospels for growing in holiness, even the deepest writings of the greatest saints and mystics.

Third, they are literary masterpieces. They take their rightful place among the classics of world literature. They need to be read and prayed with imagination and human sympathy and wonder as well as faith.

All three ways are legitimate, but not to be confused with each other.

In the Gospels, we encounter the very person and work of the Lord Jesus, the heart and the point of God's Word to us. More so than any other books of the New Testament, these four are meant to be read prayerfully and prayed biblically. Only then will everything else in God's Word, in both the Old and New Testaments, begin to make real sense.

TWO

The Gospel of the Kingdom: Matthew's Gospel

*M*ATTHEW'S GOSPEL is the first book of the New Testament, not because it was written first—some of Paul's epistles take that honor—but because it is the bridge between the Old and New Testaments. The majority of the surviving manuscripts of the Gospels or of the complete New Testament have Matthew as the first book because of this theological insight of the early Church.

For Matthew's main point and purpose in writing, the conclusion of his whole twenty-eight-chapter argument, the verdict that all 1,071 verses of evidence point to, is this: to prove to his fellow Jews that Jesus is the one all the Jewish prophets point to: the Messiah, the Christ, the King of the Jews, the founder of the kingdom of God. *Matthew's Gospel* is written by a Jew to Jews about the Jew who was crucified for claiming to be the King of the Jews.

Because Matthew was concerned about convincing the Jews, he uses far more Old Testament quotations and references than any other New Testament writer: forty direct quotations from the Old Testament and sixty other references to Jewish prophecies. Often these have the connecting phrase, "As it is written in the prophet..." or, "This was done to fulfill what was spoken by the prophets..."

That's also why Matthew refers nine times to Jesus as the "son of David." The Messiah was to be the literal descendent of David. This was very clear in the prophets.

That's also why Matthew begins with Jesus' genealogy, tracing him back to David and then to Abraham, the first Jew, through his foster-father Joseph rather than through his only biological parent Mary. In accordance with the rules of Jewish genealogy, it was the father's lineage, not the mother's, that counted legally for royalty.

That's also why Matthew introduces Jesus' public ministry with John the Baptist, who pointed to Jesus, thus fulfilling the essential task of all the prophets: to be fingers pointing to Christ. John is the last and greatest prophet of the old kingdom, the old covenant. Yet the least member of the new kingdom is to be greater than John, the greatest of the old; of that we are assured by the King himself (Mt 11:11).

John was the first prophet Scripture mentions in more than four centuries. The Word prepared his public ministry with silence—not just thirty years of silence, but over four centuries of it. Then he broke the silence and spoke the Word—himself.

John sums up the teaching of all the prophets in two words: "repent" and "believe." Jesus repeats this two-word message many times. They are the two things we absolutely need to do to be saved, to enter God's kingdom, to be justified and accepted by God, to go to Heaven, to be freed from sin, to live God's own life on earth, to be reborn by the Holy Spirit, to be in the state of grace, to become a member of Christ's mystical body. All nine of these expressions refer to the same thing, the *unum necessarium*, the "one thing needful" (Lk 10:42).

Matthew had been a tax collector for the Roman rulers. To approximate the way the Jews felt about tax collectors (publicans), imagine all the nasty lawyer jokes you have ever heard. Then add the way people feel about IRS auditors, politicians, dentists, umpires, and Mafia hit men.

Tax collectors could set their own rates over and above what their Roman masters required. Most of them lined their own pockets with extra money extorted from their own people. Thus they were regarded as both thieves and traitors. No one could have been a more unlikely convert, certainly no one a more unlikely saint.

Yet when Jesus called Matthew to follow him, he immediately left his office and his job (Mt 9:9). He had probably already heard Jesus' preaching and been moved by it. Jesus' timing was perfect, as usual. So was his choice of men. Many of the greatest saints were made out of the greatest sinners.

The fact that Matthew was one of the inner circle of twelve apostles means that *Matthew's Gospel* was written by a direct eyewitness to the events it describes (except for the narratives of Jesus' birth).

Matthew's Gospel has been called "the Gospel of the kingdom." He emphasizes the kingly aspects of Jesus, as Luke emphasizes his priestly ministry and John his prophetic wisdom.

The term "kingdom" appears fifty times, and "kingdom of heaven" thirty-two times. What is this kingdom?

It is the Church, the new Israel, where God is known and worshipped, where sins are not only forgiven but removed, where eternal life is poured out for all its citizens. This is not a political kingdom, but a spiritual one. This fact is made evident by two of the Church's recent names for herself: "the mystical (invisible) Body of Christ" (Pope Pius XII) and "the people of God" (Vatican II).

But Matthew also clearly presents Jesus as establishing a visible institution, headed by visible men. Though the Church is spiritual, not political, it is also visible—just as you are spiritual (you have a soul), yet visible.

Christ made Peter the "rock," the foundation and ruler of his Church on earth (Mt 16:13-19) after Peter confessed the reality the Church has always most centrally confessed and taught: "You are the Christ, the Son of the living God."

Jesus replied, "[For] Flesh and blood has not revealed this to you, but my Father who is in heaven." For nineteen and a half centuries the Church has always claimed that its message is from God, not from human beings, and therefore has divine authority. This claim is the fundamental scandal in the eyes of the world—the rock-hard offense that cannot be compromised. There is nothing she can do about it, for she is only God's mail carrier. She is not the author of her message and has no authority to change it, only to deliver it, to announce it, to proclaim the good news, the "deposit of faith." She *interprets* this data, but she does not edit it.

Jesus then changed Simon's name to Peter ("Rocky"). In Judaism, only God can change your name, for only God designed you and gave you your name in the first place. (Your name is not just a label but signifies your real identity.) Thus God changed Abram's name to Abraham and Jacob's name to Israel. But if an Orthodox Jew legally changed his own name, he would be excommunicated. Jesus' giving Simon a new name, then, was a claim to divinity.

After singling out Peter as the rock on which he would build his Church, he gave an incredible authority to this Church: "I will give you the keys of the kingdom of heaven, and whatever you bind (prohibit) on earth will be bound in heaven, and whatever you loose (permit) on earth will be loosed in heaven." The actions of "binding" and "loosening" in Heaven are verbs in the perfect tense, meaning that when Peter binds or loosens, it will already have been accomplished in Heaven—that is, Peter follows the will of God in Heaven and not the reverse. This is a text that should be read and prayed long and hard and honestly by "dissenters." They used to be called "heretics"—a word meaning "those who pick and choose for themselves"—just the opposite of Peter.

Jesus' last words in *Matthew's Gospel* also speak of this kingly authority. It is called the "great commission": "*All* authority in heaven and on earth has been given to me. Go therefore and make disciples of *all* the nations, baptizing them in the name of the Father and of the Son and of the Holy Spirit, teaching them to observe *all* things that I have commanded you; and lo, I am with you *always,* even to the end of the age" (Mt 28:18-19 *NKJV*, emphasis mine). Please note the four "alls."

Matthew shows Jesus' authority over *death* by his resurrection.

Matthew shows Jesus' authority over *sin* by his forgiving sins. Those who heard him claim this authority immediately perceived it as a claim to divinity; they protested, "Who can forgive sins but God alone?" (Mk 2:7).

Matthew shows Jesus' authority over *nature* by his miracles, especially the series of ten miracles he includes in chapters 8 and 9. These show his power over not only nature but disease and death as well, and even their ultimate source, the devil.

Chapter 12 is the turning point in Christ's ministry. There the Pharisees—the Jewish religious orthodoxy and national authority—reject Jesus as Messiah and even claim his power comes from the devil. After this, Christ begins to teach in parables, which his enemies do not understand; he begins to teach more to his own disciples and less in public; and he begins to emphasize his impending death.

Matthew interrupts his fast-moving narrative five times by long discourses, each ending with the set phrase "Jesus finished" (7:28; 11:1; 13:53; 19:1; 26:1). These five discourses are: (1) the "Sermon on the Mount" (ch.s 5-7), (2) missionary instructions to the disciples (ch. 10), (3) parables of the kingdom (ch. 13), (4) on the cost of discipleship (ch. 18), and (5) the Olivet discourse on the end of the world (ch.s 24-25).

This last discourse shows that the Gospel was written prior to A.D. 70 when Jerusalem was destroyed—an event Jesus *predicts* in this discourse. The event is often used by modernist Scripture scholars to "prove" that Matthew was written *after* A.D. 70. The supposition is that miracles, such as predictive prophecy, are impossible. But in that case Jesus' prophecies have been faked, and Matthew is a liar. But the scholars are seldom forthright enough to say that!

THE GREATEST SERMON EVER PREACHED

The most famous part of *Matthew* is surely the "Sermon on the Mount." It can be printed on a single page and read in fifteen minutes. Yet its influence on the world has been greater than that of any other sermon ever preached. Here is much food for prayer and reflection.

The high moral standards of this sermon have often been thought to be so impractical and impossible that it has been interpreted as a morality only for an elite circle of saints and mystics. Or it has been thought to describe how we will live in heaven, but not on earth. Finally, some consider this teaching an "interim ethic" (Albert Schweitzer's term) which could be lived only for a short time before Christ's Second Coming. In this scenario, only if we shared Christ's belief that the end was near could we live in such a detached and unselfish way. This idea that true morality must be based on a false conception of history is self-refuting.

But what *is* the right answer? The problem is the extreme difficulty of "turning the other cheek" and "going the extra mile" and avoiding hate and lust as well as murder and adultery. There are two possible solutions.

The first solution is suggested by the incident with the rich young ruler in 19:16-22. The solution is that the law is deliberately too difficult for us. Jesus is *not* giving us a morality he thinks we *can* practice, but a morality he knows we *can't*. For morality is not salvation. Morality is not the good news, the operation; it is the bad news, the diagnosis, the X-ray. It is law, not grace; law, correctly and purely interpreted.

The Pharisees had misinterpreted obedience to the moral law as a performance, as external behavior. And they obeyed it to the letter. But Jesus says that God demands more, not less, than the strict observances of the Pharisees; he demands a pure *heart*. For God is a lover, not a machine. He wants not just behavior of a certain kind but persons of a certain kind, persons who are "perfect, as your Father in heaven is perfect"

(5:48). The law shows us what we must do *and can't do.* Then and only then are we in the market for grace and salvation.

The second answer is that although we cannot, God can accomplish this tranformation in us. *Matthew* 5-7, like *1 Corinthians* 13, describes the love-life that is natural to God, not to us. It is supernatural to us. But it is what starts to happen in us when Christ gets inside.

Many modern readers dislike *Matthew's Gospel* because of its hard sayings, its warnings against riches and worldliness, its announcement of divine justice and judgment, and its demand for good works. If we dislike this book, then this is precisely the book we need most. For we need to know the whole Gospel. It is precisely those aspects of it that we still find repellant and try to avoid that we need most—not those we already understand and love.

Perhaps the most radical, challenging, life-changing passage in the whole Bible for the Christian is one of Jesus' last sayings before his trial and death, taken from the parable of the Last Judgment (25:31-46). It ends with these thought-provoking words: "Truly, I say to you, as you did it to one of the least of these my brethren, you did it to me" (v. 40). If a thousand Christians really believed that and lived accordingly, the next century would be shaped by a thousand saints.

THREE

Just the Facts: Mark's Gospel

MANY THINK THAT MARK (also called John Mark—Acts 12:25) was a good friend of St. Peter's. Peter called him "my son Mark" (1 Pt 5:13). Mark probably got his information about Jesus from Peter. Ancient writers called *Mark* "Peter's Gospel" for that reason. So even though its author was not an apostle or an eyewitness to all the events described, it is based on an eyewitness account (Peter's). It was widely known in the early Church that Mark not only translated for Peter while in Rome, but Mark also is said to have written Peter's memoirs—which many think is the *Gospel of Mark* (see Eusebius' *H.E.* 3.39.15).

Mark was probably the "young man" who was "following Jesus" mentioned in 14:51-52, the naked "streaker" in the garden. It is usual for an ancient author to mention himself anonymously in this way. Compare *John* 21:20-24.

Mark later went on missionary journeys with Paul and Barnabas, his relative (Acts 12:25; Col 4:10). He had a falling-out with Paul (Acts 13:13; 15:37-39) and was later reconciled (2 Tm 4:11). He went to Rome, like Peter and Paul, and probably wrote his Gospel there. Tradition says he was martyred in Alexandria.

Because Mark wrote for Roman readers, he omitted the things in *Matthew* that would be meaningful only to Jews, such as Jesus' genealogy, references to Old Testament prophecies (which the Romans had never read), and Jewish laws and customs that Matthew expects his reader to know. Mark also interpreted for his Latin readers some words in Aramaic, the common language of the Jews in Palestine in the time of Christ.

The ancient Romans were in many ways like modern Americans. They were a practical, pragmatic people who emphasized deeds more than words, action more than theory. They got things done. In fact, they conquered the world! Since they admired people who got things done, Mark emphasizes these aspects of Jesus, especially his miracles. After all, Jesus was, among other things, the most effective man who ever lived.

But Jesus got things done differently than the Romans did: by grace, not by force. Mark presents Jesus not as conqueror but as servant (10:45). For example, he commands the forces of nature only by being obedient to his Father's will. Though his life was filled with humble service and ministry, it was for the glory of God the Father and the salvation of his brothers and sisters: exactly our practical model for the Christian life.

The distinctive word in *Mark* is "immediately," or "at once." It occurs forty-two times. Jesus obeys his Father's will "at once." He responds to human needs "at once." The power of his love flashed out suddenly, like sunlight. (It was Sonlight.) It was "love in action," not "love in dreams" (to quote Dorothy Day's favorite line, from Dostoyevski). If we could learn just this one lesson, we would go very far toward deep personal sanctity and power to revolutionize our world. Mary did it by responding *at once*, "Be it done!" (Lk 1:38). Mark does not comment on the events he describes, or interpret their deeper meanings, like John in his Gospel. He simply gives the facts, the fast-moving events of Christ's life and death. *Mark* is *data*.

He shows how Christ's words and deeds are one, especially in his miracles. The Greek word for "miracle" means "sign." These deeds were also words, signs, and lessons. Mark includes eighteen of these "signs" in his short Gospel.

Two of the things these miraculous signs teach in *Mark* are: (1) Christ's identity as the Son of God, his divine power; and (2) his compassion and love in response to human needs. These two always go together in the Gospels. The Romans tended to separate them, to see power as unloving and love as unpowerful.

The "let's get right to the point" style of Mark is evident from the very first verse: "This is the good news about Jesus Christ, the Son of God." This is just the book for busy Romans (and busy Americans) who want the "bottom line." In the words of Police Sergeant Joe Friday of "Dragnet," "Just the facts, ma'am, if you please."

FOUR

The Great Physician: Luke's Gospel

L UKE PRESENTS JESUS AS THE GREAT PHYSICIAN, healer of bodies and souls. This emphasis was natural to him because Luke himself was a doctor.

St. Paul called Luke "our beloved physician" (Col 4:14), and a popular novel about Luke uses that title. When I think of Luke, I think of Dr. "Bones" McCoy on "Star Trek." He seems like your archetypical family doctor: down-to-earth, sensitive, compassionate, and thoroughly human.

Matthew and his Gospel seem more kingly, like Captain Kirk. John and his Gospel seem more prophetic and philosophical and mystical, like Mr. Spock. But Luke seems more priestly and more doctorly, like "Bones" McCoy. Matthew emphasizes morality and the will. John emphasizes wisdom and the mind. Luke emphasizes compassion and the feelings. To complete the "Star Trek" analogy, Mark is the practical engineer Scotty.

Not only did Luke have a doctor's "bedside manner," he also had a doctor's careful, scientific method. Since he was not himself a firsthand eyewitness to the events of Jesus' life, as Matthew and John were, he says that he "carefully studied all these matters from their beginning" (Lk 1:3) so as to write "an orderly account" of them. None of the four Gospels means to be a complete, modern-style "scientific" biography, but *Luke* comes the closest. For instance, he includes the most information about Jesus' birth and infancy, a topic Mark and John omit entirely.

Luke was not an apostle or one of Jesus' disciples because he was not a Jew, but a Gentile convert, probably a Greek. He is probably the only Gentile writer in the Bible. If we compare Colossians 4:10-11 with the following verses 12-14, we see that Paul lists him with Gentile converts rather than with Jews.

Luke wrote for Gentile readers, especially Greeks. He translates all Hebrew and Aramaic terms into Greek and explains Jewish laws, customs, and geography to his readers, assuming they are not familiar with these things. He also possessed great skill in using the Greek language—so much so, in fact, that this book has been called the most beautifully written book in the world. Greek was almost certainly his native tongue, which was not the case with Matthew, Mark, and John.

Since Luke wrote to Gentiles, he traced Jesus' genealogy all the way back to Adam, the first human being. Matthew, who wrote to Jews, traced Jesus' ancestry back to Abraham, the first Jew.

Luke accompanied Paul on at least some of his missionary journeys. When Paul thought he was near death, he wrote, "Luke alone is with me" (2 Tm 4:11)—evidence of Luke's loyalty and closeness to Paul.

Luke and *Acts* are companion books. Comparing the two prefaces (Lk 1:1-4 and Acts 1:1-5) shows clearly that they have the same author. Their style and language are also very similar. Luke's name is not mentioned in either *Luke* or *Acts*, but all the most ancient sources call this book "*the Gospel according to Luke.*"

Luke's Gospel and *Acts* were both written to Theophilus. No one knows who Theophilus was. His name means "friend of God." The title "your excellency" (Lk 1:3) indicates that he was quite powerful. He was probably also rich, for to have two books written and published was a very expensive proposition in an age when all books had to be copied by hand.

Each evangelist offers us a word picture of Jesus, the Word of God. But no two photographs of the same subject, like two reflections in a pool, are ever exactly alike due to differences in lighting, angle, speed, and composition. Each evangelist, like a photographer, highlights a different aspect of the infinite, inexhaustible, multi-faceted Christ. The aspect Luke highlights is his perfect humanity.

Thus Luke's favorite title for Jesus is "the Son of Man." His divinity is not hidden or minimized, by any means. In fact, it shines through even more clearly in the perfection of his humanity, especially his love. Luke repeatedly shows Christ's compassion for the poor, the needy, the sick, and the sorrowing. Read and pray, for example, the following Scriptures: the poor disciples (6:20); sinful women rejected by society (7:37), in particular, Mary Magdalene (8:2); the despised Samaritans (10:33); tax collectors (15:1); beggars (16:20-21); lepers (17:12); and even for the crucified, dying thief (23:43).

Luke emphasizes Jesus' sensitivity and feelings, probably because as a doctor he was himself especially sensitive to human suffering. As a doctor, Luke would also be fascinated with Jesus' miraculous healings.

The Greeks admired human perfection; they were the world's first humanists and the world's first idealists. So Luke shows Jesus as the answer to their quest, their ideal.

Luke also emphasizes grace and salvation, just as Paul does (especially in *Romans* and *Galatians*), for Luke was a close friend of Paul's and probably influenced by Paul's theological vision and emphasis. Without omitting or watering down law, justice, and judgment, Luke emphasizes God's universal grace in passages such as 2:32, 3:6 and 24:47. Compare Luke's theology of grace here with Pauline passages such as *Romans* 3:22-30 and *Ephesians* 3, and you will see the striking spiritual kinship.

Another distinctive feature of Luke is that he alone deliberately arranges everything in careful order. He is also very careful about details and about historical reliability and accuracy, showing the mind and method of a good scientific doctor and historian at work.

To my mind, the two most distinctive and attractive features of Luke's gospel are its emphasis on Mary and on the Holy Spirit. Both are mentioned far more often than in the other Gospels. The Holy Spirit is mentioned twenty-two times in *Luke*. He tells the story of Jesus' birth from Mary's point of view; Matthew tells it from Joseph's.

Mary and the Holy Spirit belong together, because they were united in spiritual marriage (see 1:35). The one who impregnated Mary and fathered Jesus was *not* Joseph but God. As the Creed says, Jesus was "conceived by the Holy Spirit, born of the Virgin Mary." Just as an ordinary human marriage is indissoluble, so is Mary's marriage to the Holy Spirit.

Another typical emphasis in *Luke* is on prayer—something that necessarily flows from both the example of Mary and the presence of the Holy Spirit, because Mary is the ideal pray-er and the Holy Spirit is the source and inspiring principle of all prayer.

Luke includes three parables on prayer not found in the other Gospels: the midnight friend (11:5-8), the unjust judge (18:1-8), and the Pharisee and publican (18:9-14). He also includes many of Christ's prayers: at his baptism (3:21), in the wilderness (5:16), before choosing his disciples (6:12), at the transfiguration (9:29), before giving us the Lord's Prayer (11:1), for Peter (22:32), in the Garden of Gethsemane (22:44), and on the cross (23:46).

Luke states Jesus' basic purpose in 19:10: "The Son of Man came to seek and to save the lost." The three parables in chapter 15 illustrate this basic point: the lost sheep, the lost coin, and the lost son (the "Prodigal Son").

The story of God's search for us, his lost children, has a beginning but no end. It continues in *Acts*, in all of history, and in present life of the Church—that is, *our* lives. This is what the Church is: God's eyes and hands searching for his

lost children. Even after he has found us, God is still searching for us in more aspects of our lives. We respond to this
search every time we pray, "Thy kingdom come."

The fundamental drama of Luke's story of this search, his
"story line," is created by human free will making its fundamental choice: will we accept God in Christ, or will we reject
him? Though Luke is "upbeat," he is also realistic and honest, and chronicles the hard-hearted human rejection of this
soft-hearted, compassionate God. As Christ reveals himself
and his claims more clearly and publicly, he is rejected all the
more.

The turning point in this drama comes in chapter 11,
when the Pharisees conclude that Jesus has (or is) a demon.
Jesus now knows that they are beyond hope since they have
committed the "unpardonable sin" (Lk 12:10)—the sin
against the Holy Spirit, the sin of deliberate, hard-hearted,
impenitent refusal of the light of truth.

Then comes the last, fatal journey to Jerusalem to die,
prefaced by the ironic "triumphal entry" on Palm Sunday.

Before he is captured and killed, Jesus gives his disciples
long instructions (which Matthew and John also recount).
The topics that Luke emphasizes in these private instructions
are: prayer, fidelity, gratitude, repentance, humility, discipleship, service, forgiveness, evangelism, and readiness for his
Second Coming. The common theme to all these topics is
that this is the business his Church is to be in. This is the
Church's business card. We would do well as members of the
Church to read these instructions prayerfully and then act on
them.

The story does not end with his death, or even with his resurrection or ascension. A new phase in the story begins with
the coming of the Holy Spirit in *Acts*. For this is "the never-
ending story." It is "the greatest story ever told." And we are
in this very same story still.

FIVE

The I AM Reveals Himself: John's Gospel

L ONGSTANDING TRADITION HAS IDENTIFIED John the author of the fourth Gospel with John "the disciple Jesus loved" (13:23; 19:26; 20:2; 21:7,20). He was the one to whom Jesus entrusted his mother when he was dying on the cross (19:26-27). He was the youngest of the apostles and lived the longest—until the time of the emperor Trajan (A.D. 98-117). We know this from Irenaeus, who was a disciple of Polycarp, who was, in turn, a disciple of John. He was one of the "inner circle" of Peter, James, and John. Most importantly, he was an eyewitness to the events he describes in his Gospel (1:14; 19:35; 21:24-25; see 1 Jn 1:1-3).

It has been a virtual touchstone of ideological acceptability in modernist theological circles to date this Gospel after John's death in the second century, and to hold that not John but "the Johannine community" wrote it. But this position is not based on any conclusive evidence in the text itself or on any evidence at all from history and the earliest tradition. It is rather based on a theological prejudice against John's "high Christology," that is, his strong emphasis on Christ's divinity. The position that this Gospel is not historically accurate because it was not written by an eyewitness (John the apostle), and that Jesus never really said the uncomfortable things this Gospel says he said—this is simply assumed and asserted as "the accepted results of modern scholarship." In my opinion, this is what students call "a snow job."

The case *for* John the apostle as author is very strong. First, the author's knowledge of Jewish customs and geography indicates that he was a Jew.

Second, his attention to numbers (2:6; 6:13; 6:19; 21:8; 21:11) and names (1:45; 3:1; 11:1; 18:10) indicates that he was a contemporary and an eyewitness, as he claims to be (1:14; 19:35; 21:24-25).

Third, he refers to himself as "the disciple Jesus loved." The other three Gospels all name Peter, James, and John as the inner circle. Peter cannot be the author because he is referred to as another person than "the disciple Jesus loved," and James cannot be the author because he was martyred too early (Acts 12:1-2). This leaves only John.

Fourth, a papyrus was discovered in Egypt (the Rylands Papyrus 52) containing parts of John 18, which has been dated to A.D. 135. This suggests a first-century date for the original Gospel, for the papyrus would have required some time to be copied and circulated.

Finally, all the early Church Fathers ascribe this Gospel to John, including Irenaeus, Clement of Alexandria, Theophilus of Antioch, and Origen.

The Gospel is arranged topically, not strictly chronologically. The central topic is the identity of Jesus. He is the great mystery man. People ask of others, "*Who* is he?" but of Jesus, "*What* is he?" They ask where he is *from*—not his home town but his home world. His startling answer is that he is from Heaven, from God. He is the most incredible thing that has ever happened: the eternal God has stepped into the world of time he created.

The identification of the man Jesus with the eternal *logos,* or divine mind, is first asserted in the magnificent, mystical prologue in chapter 1. Then it is gradually unfolded both by Jesus' *words,* which more and more clearly claim divinity, and by his *deeds,* especially his miracles.

John arranges Jesus' words around seven "I AM" statements:

1. "I AM the bread of life" (6:35,48);
2. "I AM the light of the world" (8:12; 9:5);
3. "I AM the door" (10:7,9);
4. "I AM the good shepherd" (10:11,14);
5. "I AM the resurrection and the life" (11:25);
6. "I AM the way, the truth, and the life" (14:6);
7. "I AM the true vine" (15:1-5).

"I AM" is the divine name God revealed to Moses from the burning bush (Ex 3:14). It is the name no Jew ever even pronounces, because to speak the name "I" is to claim to bear it. Exodus 3:14 is the only time God ever revealed his own essential name, as distinct from his relations and appearances to us (for example, as Lord, Creator, Father). In Hebrew, this name is called the sacred tetragrammaton or four-consonant name, JHWH. No one knows for certain how to pronounce it because the vowels were not written down and it was not spoken. The old guess was "Jehovah" and the new guess is "Yahweh." However he pronounced it, when Jesus spoke this unutterable name, claiming it for himself, he was clearly claiming divinity.

The most explicit occasion of all is in the passage 8:58: "Truly, truly I say to you, before Abraham was, I AM." The Jews' reaction to this was a clear and logical one: they tried to kill him. For if he was not God, he was the most wicked blasphemer in history and the most worthy of death. This is one of Christianity's oldest apologetic arguments: *aut deus aut homo malus:* either [he is] God or a bad man. The only thing Jesus couldn't possibly be is the very thing nearly everyone except orthodox Christians say he was: a good man, but only a man.

People are complex. There are many attitudes we can take toward any person who ever lived—except to Jesus. There are only two possible attitudes to him. John shows them emerging more and more clearly as the story unfolds, like two characters coming out of hiding. Either he is God, as he claimed to be, and must be worshiped, adored, loved, believed, and obeyed; or else he is the most dangerous liar or lunatic in history. John makes every honest reader choose between these two attitudes to Jesus because Jesus himself did exactly that.

John arranges his story of Christ's life around seven signs (miracles). Where each of the other evangelists record many miracles, John chooses only seven. But he carefully records people's reactions of belief and disbelief after each one. This culminates in the crucifixion, where unbelief seems to triumph—until Easter Sunday.

John emphasizes how Jesus was hated and rejected. He never fit people's prejudices, categories, ideologies, or set agendas. All were amazed at him. Some were enthralled and some were scandalized. Teachings like the one about eating his body and drinking his blood (6:58-69) sorted out his hearers into two camps: those who said, "This is a hard saying; who can listen to it?" (6:60) and those who said, "Lord, to whom shall we go? You have the words of eternal life" (6:68).

These are the only two camps that will ever be for all eternity. John shows us, more clearly than any other writer, the ultimate spiritual geography, the eternal map, behind the drama of belief versus unbelief. C.S. Lewis summarized the map this way: "Although there were a thousand paths by which he might walk through the world, there was not one of them that did not lead, in the end, either to the Beatific or the Miserific Vision."

The seven signs around which John organizes this drama are:

1. changing water to wine (2:1-11);
2. healing the nobleman's son (4:46-54);
3. healing the paralytic (5:1-16);
4. feeding the five thousand (6:1-13);
5. walking on the water (6:16-21);
6. healing the man born blind (9:1-7);
7. raising Lazarus from the dead (11:1-44).

These seven miracles supply the seven basic human needs, both physically and spiritually:

1. drink symbolizes joy (see Ps 104:15);
2. physical health symbolizes spiritual health (virtue);
3. physical power and mobility symbolize spiritual power;
4. bread symbolizes "the bread of life," spiritual nourishment;
5. overcoming sea and storm symbolizes faith overcoming fear;
6. physical sight symbolizes spiritual sight (wisdom);
7. resurrection from physical death symbolizes salvation from eternal death.

Thus Christ saves completely. Joy, virtue, power, life, faith, sight, and immortality replace thirst, disease, paralysis, hunger, fear, blindness, and death.

Jesus speaks much in this Gospel of eating and drinking and life and death. There are two words in Greek for "life": *bios* (natural life) and *zoe* (supernatural life). *Zoe* is the word John uses for what Jesus offers us. This is a life natural to God but supernatural to us. It includes divine power over nature via miracles, over selfishness via *agape* love, and over death via resurrection.

But no one can give what he doesn't have. The practical importance of the dogma of the divinity of Christ is this: Christ can give us supernatural life only if he has it himself, by nature. The case for Jesus' divinity is also the case for our salvation.

John presents a compelling case, including many kinds of evidence, for the incredible claim that this man of flesh and blood was God incarnate.

First, most obviously, there are his miracles. These are signs (*semeia*) of his divinity, and of our own supernatural destiny. Only a supernatural being can perform supernatural acts.

A second, even clearer sign is his resurrection. This is the final, dramatic, climactic proof of who he is. You might just come up with some natural explanation for other miracles, if you were desperate to do so, but not for conquering death. Thus John goes into greater detail about Jesus' post-resurrection appearances than the other evangelists.

A third piece of evidence is Jesus' character. It is as far as it could possibly be from that of a liar or a lunatic. He is good, wise, mature, clever, compassionate, and trustworthy. This is exactly the opposite sort of person from the madman who thinks he is God or the charlatan who dupes dumb disciples for private profit, power, and prestige, like Jim Jones or Reverend Moon.

Fourth, he forgives sins—all sins. "Who can forgive sins but God alone?"

Fifth, he changes people's lives, characters, destinies, and even their names. He changed Simon's name to Peter, something only God could do in Judaism. For your name is your self. Only God gives you that.

Insistently, repeatedly, and step by step John builds the case for Jesus' divinity and challenges each reader with his claim to be the source of eternal life. How the reader responds is literally a matter of life or death. This book is, simply, the most important book ever written. It is the book of life. It is a book we should read and pray again and again.

No book lays it out more plainly. John tells us explicitly why he wrote his Gospel in 20:31. (How can so many scholars *discuss* the issue, as if there were some secret code or hidden agenda only the scholars knew?) It is the Gospel in a nutshell:

"... [T]hese things are written that you might believe that Jesus is the Christ, the Son of God, and that believing you may have life (*zoe*) in his name."

SIX

The Gospel of the Holy Spirit: The First Part of Acts

CHRISTIANS IN THE FIRST CENTURY were called "these men who have turned the world upside down" (Acts 17:6). How did they do it? How can we do it again?

The Acts of the Apostles is like a mystery and adventure novel. The mystery is how twelve men who were mostly peasants and fishermen changed the world more than any other group has ever done. What was their secret? The adventure moves through life and death situations, black magic, real miracles, murder, shipwreck, trials, torture, stoning, prison, earthquake, encounters with angels, conspiracy, and conversion. It leaves you breathless, like an Indiana Jones movie.

Two of the three main characters are Sts. Peter and Paul. Peter was the first pope, the "Rock" on which Christ promised to build his Church. Paul was like a whirlwind. He was the greatest missionary of all time. No person ever did more to Christianize the world than Paul. If we need more rocks and whirlwinds in the Church today, maybe we should go back to this book for our models.

But the main character in *Acts* is Jesus Christ. *Acts* is a continuation of *Luke's Gospel* (read Lk 1:1-4; then Acts 1:1). Just as the Gospel is the story of Christ, *Acts* is the story of the Body of Christ, the Church.

This book brings us back to basics. It shows us what the

Church most basically is: a conspiracy of love for a dying world, a spy mission into enemy-occupied territory ruled by the powers of evil, a prophet from God with the greatest news the world has ever heard, the most life-changing and most revolutionary institution that has ever existed on earth.

The Church is not just a human institution. It is not just an organization but an organism. Just as your body is not simply a bunch of cells, the Church is not simply a collection of human beings. Just as your soul is the life of your body, the Holy Spirit is the life of the Church.

Acts has been called "the Gospel of the Holy Spirit." That's why after Jesus' ascension it begins with Pentecost, the birth-day of the Church, the coming of the Holy Spirit. That same Spirit is the secret power that turned murderers into martyrs and sinners into saints. He planned and directed the whole plot of *Acts*. He empowered and inspired its human actors. The Holy Spirit is the real hero of the story. (Yes, "he," not "it." He's a person, like the Father and the Son, not a "force.")

The first part of *Acts* tells the story of the Church in the East, in Jerusalem and Antioch. The storyline centers on Peter, the apostle to the Jews. The second part tells of the Church in the Roman West and centers on Paul, the apostle to the Gentiles. Together these two great saints-martyrs-evangelists-missionaries are the joint "pillars of the Church."

Luke, the author, was Paul's companion on his missionary journeys around the Roman world. That's why he often uses "we" (for example, see Acts 16, 20, and 27). The action begins in Jerusalem, where Christianity began with Peter's first sermon, and ends in Rome, the center of the ancient world, with Paul, a visitor in the emperor's household, making converts everywhere and waiting to be martyred.

How is this story of ancient times relevant to us and our world today? Our world is just as corrupt, just as hard and proud, just as violent, just as needy, as the world was then. This book gives us the pattern for turning it upside down again.

We have the same Church, the same power source (the Holy Spirit), the same good news, and the same last orders from our Lord, "Go therefore and make disciples of all nations" (Mt 28:19). No force on earth can stop us except our own laziness and lack of faith.

We need to recapture the faith, hope, and forward-looking optimism of the apostles in *Acts*. Then we too can perform the same "acts of the apostles." After Jesus left them and ascended to Heaven, you would think they would now look back to the past, the glorious time when he had been with them. But no, they looked to the future, for the future was to be even more glorious. Jesus himself had told them that it would be better for them if he left and sent them the Holy Spirit (Jn 16:7).

How could this be *better*? Wouldn't it be better if we had Jesus still physically, humanly present? No. When he was here, his disciples still misunderstood him. Only when he sent the Spirit could they begin the tremendous tasks narrated in this book.

Why? Because God the Father is *outside* us, and God the Son *beside* us, but God the Holy Spirit is *inside* us. This is only a view of the *roles* of the three persons of the Godhead. Of course, there are not three Gods—one outside us, one inside us, and one beside us.

Being *inside* another is maximum intimacy. Intimacy is what love aims at, and God is love. The whole Bible is the love story between God and his people, his Church. *Acts* begins the third and last and most intimate stage of all.

The Church is the most powerful force on earth not only because she has the highest ideal above her, but above all because she has the greatest power within her. This book shows us what that power can accomplish.

THE HOLY SPIRIT, THE CHURCH'S POWER SOURCE

Acts begins with Jesus' ascension. But this is not the end of the story. It is the beginning. With a sense of mounting excitement, the reader turns, like the apostles, from the departing Jesus to the coming Holy Spirit.

The physical presence of Jesus wasn't enough. If the Holy Spirit hadn't come, Christians could never have won the world. Here is shocking evidence for that, in the form of one of the stupidest questions ever asked. After teaching his apostles for forty days the meaning of his kingdom (1:3), Jesus gets this question: "Lord, will you at this time restore the kingdom to Israel?" (1:6). In other words, "Your kingdom *is* a political kingdom, a this-worldly kingdom, isn't it? Are we finished with all this spiritual stuff now and can we get down to the 'bottom line' of kicking out those awful Romans and liberating our nation? That's what you came for, right?"

Not until the Spirit came did they understand. Not until the Spirit came did they have the spiritual power to win hearts and minds. Jesus knew that. That's why he told them *not* to go out to all the world and preach the Gospel, not yet (1:4-5). That would have been like trying to pull a plow with a kitten, or light up a city with a flashlight. There's a power shortage.

The Spirit is as necessary as Jesus. The Spirit is like a plug, Jesus is like electricity in the wires, and the Father is like the dynamo that generates the electricity. You need to plug into the power. Having an ideal, a blueprint, without the power to live it produces only a sense of failure, frustration, and guilt. Only God the Holy Spirit can empower us to live the life that God the Son lived and God the Father commanded.

That is the secret of the Church. That is the reason for her staying power, her enduring through centuries of persecution, her saints and martyrs, her profundity of doctrine, her infallibility and consistency throughout two thousand years. Nothing but God working inside her, not just outside her or beside her, nothing less than God the Holy Spirit as the soul of the Church, could perform this miracle in history.

Thus, this book, which is a history of the early Church, begins with Pentecost, the descent of the Holy Spirit. Pentecost is the birthday of the Church. Just as God breathed his Spirit into Adam and turned mere "dust of the earth" into a man (Gn 2:7), so he again breathed his Spirit into a band of confused, weak human beings and turned them into the one and only thing on this earth that the gates of Hell themselves will never prevail against, the one thing we can be certain will last until the end of time: the Church, Christ's own new Body.

You see the change the Holy Spirit makes most strikingly in Peter. Read all the passages in the four Gospels that refer to Peter, and you will see how confused and weak he is. Then read all the passages in *Acts*, beginning with his Pentecost sermon, that mention Peter. You see a new man, a real Rock for the first time.

His impromptu sermon on Pentecost converted three thousand people (2:41). It was so effective that after it was over, his listeners asked not, What should we think? but, What should we do? (2:37). When the great orator Cicero make a speech before the Roman senate, all the senators said, "How well he speaks!" But they remained seated. When the great general Demosthenes addressed his Greek troops, they stood up, clashed their swords upon their shields, and shouted, "Let us march!" Peter is now like Demosthenes, not Cicero.

Peter's answer to their question, "What shall we do?" summarizes the whole Bible, all three parts of God's plan for our redemption. First, the Old Testament prophets, culminating in John the Baptist, focus on one thing: "Repent." Turn away from sin and back to God. Second, the Gospels show us the way to be incorporated into Christ and receive his forgiveness: "And be baptized, every one of you, in the name of Jesus Christ for the forgiveness of your sins." But there is a third part too: "And you shall receive the gift of the Holy Spirit" (2:38).

Then, as if he were looking over the heads of his immediate audience and down the centuries to us, he added, "For the promise (of the Holy Spirit) is to you *and to your children and to all that are far off, every one whom the Lord our God calls to him*" (2:39, emphasis mine).

A poor European family was immigrating to America. They had saved for years to buy the tickets. The only food they had with them for the journey was bread and cheese. After a few days, the little boy said to his father, "I can't stand this any more. Nothing but cheese sandwiches. Please give me some money for some real food." The father gave him his last nickel and told him to buy something in the ship's dining room. The boy came back in two hours, fat and happy. "I had soup and steak and ice cream and pie. It was great!" "What?" the father asked. "Did you buy all that with a nickel?" "Oh, no, Dad. The food's free. It comes with the ticket."

The Church today is surviving on cheese sandwiches. The Holy Spirit is steak and pie. He's part of the package deal, part of God's plan for us. He comes with the ticket. The great things the Church accomplished in *Acts* can be done in our day, if we only had the power. That power is available for the asking. Read and pray *Luke* 11:5-13.

PETER, THE FIRST POPE, AND STEPHEN, THE FIRST MARTYR

Acts tells the dramatic story of the early Church—a Church that was very poor in material wealth and power, but very rich in spiritual wealth (full of saints and martyrs) and power (miracles).

At other times in the Church's history, especially the Renaissance, it was just the reverse. The Church had amassed great worldly wealth, but it had gotten weak and corrupt. That contrast is the point of the story of a Renaissance pope who was proudly showing a saintly friend all the riches of his treasury. "See?" he said, "Peter can no longer say, 'I have no silver or gold.'" "No," replied the friend, "But neither can he say, 'In the name of Jesus, rise and walk!'"

The pope and his friend were referring to the story in *Acts* 3. Peter and John, newly filled with the power of the Holy Spirit at Pentecost, go into the temple and see a man who had been lame from birth. The man was begging for money, but instead of material wealth he found spiritual wealth in Peter, who said to him, "I have no silver or gold, but what I have, I give you: In the name of Jesus Christ of Nazareth, rise up and walk!"—and the man rose and walked.

The Renaissance pope said, "*Peter* can no longer say, 'I have no silver or gold'" because the chain of popes stretches back to Peter, whom Christ appointed. When he said, "... [O]n this rock I will build my church..." (Mt 16:18).

But the name "Peter" does not seem to fit him in the Gospels. It means "rock," but Peter is hardly "Rocky" before Pentecost. He is more like "Sandy." Peter is weak and vacillating, misunderstanding Christ, making mistakes (like fighting with his sword in the Garden of Gethsemane), and cowardly (denying Christ three times during his trial). Naming him "Rocky" is a joke, like naming a skinny man "Fats."

Yet in *Acts* Peter fulfills Jesus' prophecy about his name. He becomes a real rock. He leads the infant Church through persecutions, uncertainties, and hard times (let's not romanticize the early Church!), just as all his successors have done. (Only later were they called *popes.*)

Acts centers first on Peter. Then, beginning with chapter 9, it focuses on Paul. In both parts, we see the Church growing in the face of problems that would have destroyed any merely human institution.

Peter's boldness in *Acts* contrasts strikingly with his former cowardice. He dares to say straight out to the people who called for Jesus' crucifixion—and who might well have called for Peter's too—"[You] killed the Author of life" (3:15). But he adds, "I know that you acted in ignorance" (3:17). When commanded by the authorities to stop preaching the Gospel, he answered, "We must obey God rather than men" (5:29), and "... we cannot but speak of what we have seen and heard" (4:20). His message is clear and uncompromising: "... there is salvation in no one else, for there is no other name under heaven given among men by which we must be saved" (4:12).

Everyone wondered at Peter and the other apostles, just as they had wondered at Jesus. "Now when they saw the boldness of Peter and John, and perceived that they were uneducated, common men, they wondered, and they recognized that they had been with Jesus" (4:13). Everyone who met Jesus wondered at him: his friends (whose wonder turned to worship), his enemies (whose wonder turned to bitter hatred), and those who just didn't know what to think. The wonder of Jesus now rubs off onto the apostles.

In chapters 6 and 7, we find the story of Stephen, the first Christian martyr. Wherever Christianity is strong, there have always been martyrs; wherever there have been Christian martyrs, Christianity has been strong. "The blood of the martyrs is the seed of the church," said Tertullian, a prominent thinker of the early Church.

It's not that Christianity teaches that you should seek out martyrdom, but that whenever the world sees great Christians, it fears and even hates them, as the decayed tooth hates and fears the dentist, or the cancer fears the surgeon.

Jesus promised, many times, in the Gospels, that his followers would be hated, persecuted, and martyred, just as he was (see Jn 15:18-20; 16:33; 16:2; 17:14; Lk 6:22; Mt 10:22; 24:9).

In those parts of the world in which the Church has been persecuted in this century, she has become very strong: China, Russia, Poland, former East Germany, and Czechoslovakia. But wherever being a Catholic is easy, the Church becomes weak: France, Holland, England, former West Germany, America, and even Italy.

After fifty years of China welcoming Christian missionaries (1905-1956), there were only two million converts. But after thirty years of persecution under Mao Tse Tung, there were an estimated twenty million Christians in China by 1986.

The martyr Stephen does not mince words or beg for mercy. He sounds like an Old Testament prophet (see 7:51-53). Yet as he dies under the stoning of the Jewish leaders in Jerusalem, he prays, "Lord, do not hold this sin against them" (7:60), just as Jesus prayed on the cross, "Father, forgive them" (Lk 23:34). This combination of toughness and love runs throughout the Bible, for it is what God himself is like: neither wimpy nor nasty. The apostles are like Jesus now, for they are filled with *his* Spirit. This is the power that fueled the Church like a rocket ship through history.

SEVEN

The Gospel Is Preached to the Gentiles: The Second Part of Acts

THE CONVERSION OF PAUL (ACTS 9)

What happened in *Acts* 9 is crucial for the history of the Church and the world that it was about to convert and change. It is the conversion of Paul, the greatest Christian missionary of all time, the one who more than any other single individual after Christ was responsible for converting half the world. Most of the rest of *Acts* is about him, and most of the rest of the New Testament after *Acts* is written by him (13 or 14 epistles). This chapter tells how he became Paul.

His name had been Saul. God changed his name to Paul. As we saw with Peter, only God can change your name, for the ancient Jews did not think of a name as a mere label given by parents, but as signifying your real, true identity, which only God can give you.

Like Abram (Abraham), Jacob (Israel), Simon (Peter) and Saul (Paul), we all are destined to have a new name if we are on the road to Heaven (see Rv 2:17). This is a name we do not yet know; only God knows it. Do you think the change that happened to Saul on earth in *Acts* is incredible? You are destined for an even greater change in Heaven.

Let's look at Saul before his conversion first, since the rest of *Acts* centers on Paul after his conversion.

The first thing we learn about him is that he was present at the stoning of Stephen, the first Christian martyr (ch. 7). He watched the coats of the men who stoned Stephen. And he consented to his death (8:1).

The next thing we hear is that he "was ravaging the church, and entering house after house, he dragged off men and women and committed them to prison" (8:3). The "dragging" was literal. The fact that he also put women in prison was especially cruel and unusual.

We would call this man a "religious fanatic" and "bigot"— someone like the Ayatollah Khomeini—and probably dismiss him as hopelessly wicked. But that just shows how different our thinking is from God's. God picks out this man to become an apostle, a missionary, and a saint.

Why did God select this man? First, God always surprises us. Throughout the Bible, he never does the expected. He often chooses what seems foolish in the eyes of the world to shame the worldly-wise (see 1 Cor 1 on this, especially v. 27). We need to learn that God's work does not fit into human expectations. Also no one, however hate-filled and bigoted, is hopeless. If God can convert and save a murderer, do you think your sins are too much for him to handle?

Second, a religious fanatic at least has passion. He's moving in the wrong direction, but at least he's moving. It's easier to move a car to the right if it's already moving to the left than if it's not moving at all.

God never made a saint out of a wimp. He wants lovers because he is love. He wants not wrongly directed love, but he does want love, not laid-back, "cool," blasé, detached, uncaring laziness.

At the beginning of chapter 9, we find Saul "still breathing threats and murder against the disciples." But on his way to Damascus to search for Christians to throw into prison, he is literally knocked off his high horse: "Suddenly a light from heaven flashed about him. And he fell to the ground and heard a voice saying to him, 'Saul, Saul, why do you persecute me?' And he said, 'Who are you, Lord?' And he said, 'I am Jesus, whom you are persecuting'" (9:3-5).

Saul must have been absolutely and totally dumbfounded. He had thought he was serving God and doing God's will by persecuting Christians. He had thought Christians were the worst blasphemers in the world, because they worshiped a human being who claimed to be God. Now God—the God Saul served with misdirected passion—speaks to him and says he is persecuting *him!*

When Saul humbly asked, 'Who are you, Lord?' that may well have been the first time in his life he admitted a mistake. (Fanatics are not usually humble.) And what a mistake! He didn't even know who God was—the God he worshiped and served, the God in whose name he was persecuting Christians. Saul suddenly gets an open mind. And into that opening steps Christ.

Notice the amazing fact that Jesus said to Saul that Saul was persecuting *him*, even though Jesus was now ascended and in Heaven. For Saul was persecuting the Church. What a dramatic way to learn the identity of Christ and his Church!

When Paul later wrote in *Ephesians* 5 that Christ is the "head" and the Church is his "body," he meant this just as truly as the thing between your ears is your head and the thing it is perched on top of is your body.

Jesus had said to his disciples, "Truly, I say to you, as you did it not to one of the least of these my brethren, you did it not to me" (Mt 25:45). "Truly, I say to you" is a formula for "I really mean this, don't water this down, it's no exaggeration." So when we snub or exploit or abort our fellow human being, we snub or exploit or abort Jesus Christ.

Paul's conversion did not take him out of the war he had been fighting, but it put him on the other side and changed the weapons from physical to spiritual ones and from hatred to love. Christ chose Paul to suffer for him rather than inflict suffering (9:16). Shortly after he is converted, those who had commissioned him to kill Christians (9:2) try to kill him (9:23).

To be converted is to become more like Christ. Christ did not fight, but he did not avoid a fight either. He went right into the center of the fight—where good and evil cross—and suffered on that cross. Now Paul is ready to follow him.

Are we?

If you were brought to trial on the charge of being a Christian, would there be enough evidence to convict you?

HOW BIG IS CHRISTIANITY?: ACTS 10-15

We take for granted today that Christianity is universal, for everyone. *Acts* 10-15 shows how this was not so obvious at first to the early Christians. Most of them were Jews. Judaism had always been a special divine revelation, for Jews only. We do not realize what a great shock it was to realize that now, for the first time in history, the knowledge of the true God was to spread throughout the whole world.

Orthodox Jews, who believe in a real messiah to come, do not prosyletize or send out missionaries to make converts, because their Old Testament prophets said that the knowledge of God was to "cover the earth as the waters cover the sea" *only* when the Messiah comes. And they do not believe that the Messiah has come yet. (Jews who are not Orthodox do not usually believe in a literal messiah, and they do not prosyletize either, but for other reasons.)

God had to teach this surprising new truth of Christianity's worldwide destiny to the two "pillars of the Church," Peter and Paul, in dramatic ways. He knocked Paul off his horse and shone a great light from Heaven on him to show him that Christianity was not a heretical sect but the truth for everyone (ch. 9). The fact that God would now reveal himself to everyone, Gentiles as well as Jews, through Christ was so shocking to Paul that he called it a great "mystery" in *Ephesians* 1:9-10 and 3:3-6.

God had to shatter *Peter's* narrowness too. He did this by sending him a strange vision (ch. 10) of a great sheet let down from Heaven with both kosher and non-kosher animals in it, commanding him to eat them all, contrary to Jewish dietary laws. The age of the law was over; Christ had begun the age of grace.

Even though it was not easy for Peter to change his lifelong habits, he was open to God's leading (10:28-29, 34-35; 11:17) because he had been filled with the Holy Spirit at Pentecost. Peter now follows where his master leads. Ever since this first pope, the Spirit has led the popes, and through them the Church, where he wants it to go.

Catholics have a single, visible Church. From the beginning, the single, central, and visible Church has had authority over all Christians. This is evident in *Acts* 15 when the question came up of whether Gentile converts had to be circumcised and made Jews before they could be baptized and made Christians (see 15:5-6, 22-30). Peter clearly assumed a leading role and was the main speaker at this first Church council. Their decision is expressed in words claiming divine, not just human authority: "it seemed good to the Holy Spirit and to us" (v. 28). From the beginning, there was one Church for the whole world.

Also from the beginning there were divisions and disputes within the Church. Paul and Barnabas were good men (see 11:24; 15:37-40), yet they had an angry argument and separated. Internal divisions are much harder for the Church to endure than external persecutions. Yet she endures both, for even the gates of Hell will never prevail against the Church Jesus built on the rock (Mt 16:18).

In chapter 12 King Herod kills James and imprisons Peter. But God has other plans for Peter, and no human force can confine God's plans. An angel frees Peter from prison, just as *Psalm* 91:11 and *Revelation* 3:7-8 promise.

This same wicked King Herod is struck dead when he blasphemously accepts the title of "a god" (Acts 12:21-23), just as Ananias and Sapphira were struck dead in chapter 5 when they lied to God. The armies of the supernatural world, both good and evil, are encountered in these extraordinary incidents, breaking through into our world. Another example of this is Elymas the Sorcerer (13:8-11), whose spiritual blindness breaks out in physical blindness. These are not fanciful myths but real miracles, told in a matter-of-fact, eyewitness style.

Acts is the history of a spiritual warfare between supernatural good and evil, Christ and the Antichrist, powers from Heaven and Hell. The spiritual war becomes physical when Christians are persecuted. For instance, Paul is stoned almost to death (14:19) and later imprisoned (ch. 16).

Does the Gospel produce such reactions today? Indeed it does—at least wherever the true Gospel is preached, instead of some mild, popular, watered-down part of it.

Almost no one hates or persecutes you if you preach those parts of the Gospel that are popular today, such as peace, justice, compassion, and social action. But you are often hated and rejected today if you dare to say such unpopular things as these:

- that Jesus is not just one among many equal religious figures, but the only true God;
- that sin, judgment, and Hell are real;
- that sexual sins, like other sins, are really sins and need to be repented of and turned away from;
- that Christianity is not a moral fable but a supernatural, miraculous fact;
- that there is objective truth and objective values, that people can be wrong, that "true for me" isn't enough.

The methods of persecution have changed. They don't stone believers today. They ostracize them socially and censor them in the media. The media (especially the movies) nearly always portray Christians as bigoted, rigid, harsh, intolerant, narrow-minded, and stupid. These are some of the stones thrown today: word-stones. But they cannot kill the truth, just as they couldn't kill Paul. Media censorship can't imprison the truth, just as Peter (ch. 12) and Paul and Silas (ch. 16) could not be imprisoned. When God opens doors, no one can close them.

God opened Gentile doors only after he gave the Jews the first opportunity. Wherever Paul went, he preached the Gospel first to the Jews (see Rom 1:16). *Acts* 13 tells how he did this at Antioch, showing how Jesus fulfilled the Jewish prophets, Jewish Scriptures, and Jewish history. A Jew who accepts Jesus as the Messiah today, just as in the first century, does not become a Gentile but a completed Jew.

But Paul's hearers reacted with envy and tried to kill him. In the first century, Jews in authority sometimes tried to kill Christians. Once Christians became part of the power structure, they often tried to kill Jews. No one has a monopoly on evil.

It was ironic that most first-century Jews rejected Christ while many Gentiles accepted him, for God had entrusted his most complete revelation to the Jews. They should have known God better than anyone else and recognized Christ, for "like Father, like Son" (see Jn 8:19; 5:39).

ACTS 17: HOW CHRISTIANITY WENT WEST

Acts 17 tells us why we in the Western world know about Christianity today, as most of the Orient does not. It tells the dramatic story of why Christianity went to Europe rather than Asia—an event that changed the next two thousand years of world history.

It also tells the story of the first meeting of Christianity and Greek philosophy. These were the two strongest and most long-lasting spiritual forces in the ancient world. They are the two forces that have continued to influence the Western world more than any other. And they are the two forces from the ancient world that met and married and made the next great era of history, the Middle Ages.

The Holy Spirit was directing history by directing the apostles. In *Acts* 13:2, Luke writes, "The Holy Spirit said, 'Set apart for me Barnabas and Saul (Paul) for the work to which I have called them.'" Notice how real and personal the Holy Spirit is. He is not just a force but a real divine person, who speaks and commands specifically and concretely. If the apostles had not been open and obedient to him, God's plan for human history would not have been fulfilled. God uses human instruments; we the Church are his hands and feet.

In *Acts* 16:6, Luke writes that they had "been forbidden by the Holy Spirit to speak the word in Asia." ("Asia" here means what was called "Asia Minor", that is, modern Turkey.) If the apostles had insisted on their own plans instead of following the Holy Spirit, they would have gone East with the Gospel instead of West. If they had done that, Europe would probably have remained pagan, Asia rather than Europe and America would have become the Christian continent, and we would probably not be Christians today.

This didn't happen, because Paul obeyed a dream God sent him, the "Macedonian vision": "... a vision appeared to Paul in the night: a man of Macedonia [northern Greece] was standing beseeching him and saying, 'Come over to Macedonia and help us.' And when he had seen the vision, immediately we sought to go into Macedonia, concluding that God had called us to preach the gospel to them" (16:9-10).

So Paul worked his way down through northern Greece to Athens, the capital city and the home of Greek culture and philosophy. Here now for the first time, the two great forces of Christianity and Greek philosophy meet.

Athens was full of idols, and this "provoked" Paul (ch. 16). The whole ancient world, except for the Jews and the Christians, worshiped false gods (idols) and many gods (polytheism). Yet even here, Paul is able to make a positive point of contact.

The reason this could happen and the reason the Gospel

took root there, was because the Athenians were genuinely seeking the truth. They were honest, open-minded, and "devout" people (see 17:11-12, 17).

So when the philosophers (17:18) asked Paul to preach to them (17:20), Paul began by praising them for being "very religious" (17:22). Though their theology was wrong and idolatrous, their hearts were honest and seeking the truth.

In contrast, when Paul wrote to the Christians in Corinth, Greece's second city after Athens, he severely criticized them for their pride and arrogance, even though their theology was much more correct than the theology of the Athenian pagans.

Like Jesus, Paul gave his different audiences what each really needed. Humble and ignorant truth-seekers like the Athenians need encouragement and knowledge. Proud know-it-alls like the Corinthians need a dose of humility and even insult (see 1 Cor 1:18-3:23).

In fact, what Paul says in *1 Corinthians* 3:18 is almost exactly what the wisest, best, and most famous Greek philosopher Socrates had taught four hundred years earlier: true wisdom consists in recognizing that we are *not* wise. Some of the philosophers Paul preached to in Athens had learned that Socratic spirit of humility and thirsting for truth. Now finally their thirst was about to be quenched.

Socrates had been a stonecutter. He may have actually cut the very words Paul referred to in *Acts* 17:23 on the altar "To an unknown god", for he believed in one single God whom he did not claim to name or define, unlike most other Greeks, who believed in many gods, like Zeus and Athena.

Here now is the point of contact, like two wires crossing. Paul says something astonishing in 17:23: "The god you worship in ignorance, I now declare to you." Paul says that these Socratic, God-seeking Greek pagans were already worshiping the true God just by seeking him, even though they did not know him.

Incidentally, this is a very strong reason for believing that pagans can be saved. As Christ promised, all who seek, find (Mt 7:8).

First Paul approves the Athenians' initial step: admitting they did not know God and seeking him. Then he takes them to the second step: he tells how God made himself known to the Jews as the one supreme, perfect Creator and Father. Finally, he tells them about God incarnate, Christ the Son. It is a natural three-stage teaching that can be used as effectively with modern post-Christian pagans, as it was used with ancient pre-Christian pagans by Paul.

It works because what was said by Pascal, the great seventeenth century Christian philosopher, is true: "There are only three kinds of people: those who have sought God and found Him and now serve Him; those who neither seek Him nor find Him; and those who are busy seeking Him but have not yet found Him. The first are reasonable and happy, the second are unreasonable and unhappy, the third are reasonable but unhappy." The Athenians were in the third class. They were reasonable and wise because they were seeking, but not yet happy because they had not yet found him.

Everyone in the third class eventually gets into the first, unless Christ's promise is a lie. But no one from the second class gets into the first. Only those who seek God, want God, and love God, find him. We are saved by our love, not our knowledge, by our hearts being open to God. The pagan Western world was seeking God. That's why it found God and was converted. The modern world can be reconverted too. All it has to do is seek, as honestly and humbly as the ancient Greeks, and the story of *Acts* can come alive again today.

EIGHT

The Church in Acts and the Church Today

W HAT'S THE DIFFERENCE between the Church in *Acts* and the Church today?

Essentially, nothing. It's the same Church: the Church Christ founded, the Church that teaches with his authority ("He who hears you, hears me..." Lk 10:16), the Church to whom he promised that the gates of Hell and the power of death would never prevail against her (Mt 16:18).

But compared with the Church in *Acts*, there seems to be a spiritual power shortage today. When Paul asked the Christians in Ephesus, "Did you receive the Holy Spirit when you believed?" (19:2), he must have seen something missing there. I think he would ask us the same question today.

How do we stack up? Let's detail some of the specific results of the Holy Spirit directing the Church in *Acts*. Keep in mind that this is supposed to be normal, not abnormal.

1. The Spirit is heard personally, directly, and concretely as a person (see 21:4 and 23:11). He is not just an *object* of belief. He certainly is not thought of merely as a vague idea or force. How many of us know him personally today?

2. Miracles are done so powerfully through Paul that even his handkerchiefs are an agency for healing (19:11-12)! The promises Christ made in the Gospels (see Mark 16:18) are lit-

erally fulfilled. For example, in *Acts* 28:3-6 Paul is bitten by a poisonous scorpion on Malta and is unharmed. How many miracles have happened in your parish lately?

3. Demonic activity appears (19:13-19), and exorcism is needed, for the devil does not sit idly by when heavenly forces march boldly into spiritual battle. How many of our clergy are trained to be exorcists?

4. Confession, repentance, and turning away from sin are clear and strong (19:18-19). Today when the idea of spiritual warfare is largely forgotten among Catholics, the practice of confession is infrequent and the sense of sin is weak.

5. The faith is so strong that unbelievers are offended. Spiritual warfare erupts as visible troubles, even riots (ch. 21). Why? No one feels threatened by a vague, wimpy faith. But the idol-makers in Ephesus were threatened by the Church's uncompromising condemnation of idolatry (19:23 ff).

Today, the enemies of God fear his Church only when she speaks boldly against modern idolatries, whether of sexual immorality, or of "freedom of choice" to murder unborn babies, or materialistic consumerism, or trusting in war to solve international problems. The true faith in its fullness is bound to offend unbelievers. Christ is like chemotherapy that threatens a cancer. Worldliness fears holiness (see 24:25).

6. Worship is such a joy that long services are common. In *Acts* 20, Paul preaches so long that a young man, Eutychus, falls asleep, falls out of a window, and dies. (God uses Paul to bring him back to life.) When did you last attend a two-hour Mass?

7. Christians are ready to die as martyrs (21:13). In the next few centuries, many *were* martyred. They were willing to die for Christ because they had found Christ more precious than life itself (see Phil 3:8). Can we say the same?

8. The "good news" is preached as historical fact, not mere "values"; and as *present* fact, not just past. Paul's speech at Jerusalem to the Jews who wanted to kill him (ch. 22) and his speech to the pagan king Agrippa (ch. 26) both center not on theology or ethics or argument, but personal testimony.

He shares how he met Jesus.

Today, fundamentalist churches are growing many times faster than the Catholic Church, especially in Latin America, largely because of this kind of appeal. You can't argue with the facts of changed lives.

9. The faith is not politicized, as it often is today. All political factions, left and right, are threatened and conspire against Paul. All the "powers that be" hate him for he serves not one of them, but a Higher Power. The true Church is neither the "establishment" nor a political "liberation" movement.

10. The Church is bold. Paul could have saved himself if he hadn't appealed to Caesar (25:12; 26:32), but he goes right to the top, refusing no risk and no task. He has total confidence, for "If God is for us, who is against us?" (Rom 8:31). He speaks directly, powerfully, without subtle "nuancing", like modern theologians, and without worrying about being "acceptable," like modern "Catholic" politicians (see 26:24-29).

11. Prophecies abound, and the Church is open to them (see 27:10,22; vv. 31 and 34). Have you heard any good prophecies lately?

12. Angels interact with humans (5:19; 8:26; 10:3; 12:7-11; 27:23), just as happened in the Old Testament, as recounted by Paul (7:30,35,38). This is part of the "package deal." Angels are real, not myths or symbols. Did you ever meet anyone who had met an angel?

13. Though tiny, the Church is famous, even notorious, just as Jesus was (28:22). They had "turned the world upside down" (17:6). They were "countercultural" and feared no earthly establishment, for they served God, not a human power structure (5:29).

And we today? Are we turning the world upside down? Or is it turning us upside down?

Acts is meant to be not dead, rusty history but a pattern for the Church in all times, including the present time. Just as Stephen treated Moses' life not as dead history but as God's pattern of action which was being repeated in his own day (ch. 7), so we are meant to repeat in our day the acts of *Acts*.

It can happen again, if only we want it. St. Francis of Assisi said, "Tell me, who do you think is the readier: God to give grace, or we to receive it?"

Not only *can* it happen again, but I think it *will* happen again. I think it is already beginning to happen again. Part of the reason is that our present pope is in many ways like St. Paul.

His whole religious life centers on the person of Christ, meeting Christ, obeying Christ.

He has travelled around the world like a missionary.

He has performed exorcisms (two at the Vatican).

He speaks boldly and plainly, offending his enemies.

He is ready to die as a martyr. He lived under Nazi and Communist persecution in Poland. He was shot and nearly killed.

When he preaches, he appeals to experience, not just theory.

He has experienced prophecies and healings, and other charismatic gifts of the Spirit.

I do not know whether he has ever seen an angel. But I would not be surprised.

Let us pray that God has raised up a second Paul to help convert the world a second time. For our civilization, like ancient Rome, is dying. Nothing can carry us through the second Dark Ages, into which we are moving, except the power that carried us through the first.

NINE

The Church's Treasure Trove of Wisdom: Introduction to the Epistles

I N *THE ACTS OF THE APOSTLES* we glimpsed a slice of the early history of the Church whose apostles wrote the New Testament. The natural next step would be to read the writings of those apostles: the twenty-one epistles or letters in the New Testament. Most of their authors and recipients are mentioned in *Acts*. *Acts* is *about* the apostles, the epistles are *by* the apostles.

Both the Old and New Testaments are divided into three parts: books of history, wisdom literature, and prophecy. (That's the order in the Table of Contents.) The epistles are the New Testament's "wisdom literature," corresponding to *Job, Psalms, Proverbs, Ecclesiastes,* and *The Song of Solomon* in the Old Testament. While history focuses on the past and prophecy on the future, wisdom literature deals with eternal truths for all time.

Paul, the greatest missionary apostle, wrote the most epistles: thirteen, from *Romans* through *Philemon.* He and other apostles wrote many other letters too (some are mentioned in these epistles), but they are all lost. These twenty-one are the ones God providentially chose to preserve for us.

Romans comes first because it is the longest and also the

most important for two reasons: (1) it was written to Christians in Rome, the capital of the world; and (2) it is the world's first systematic, logically organized, Christian theology. Ever since, every orthodox Christian theologian has elaborated the same two essential themes as *Romans:* sin and salvation, the "bad news" and the "good news." Chapter 8 is, I think, the very best news, the most exalted and joyful chapter ever written.

First Corinthians offers an intimate look at many specific serious problems in this local church: factions, lawsuits, incest, divorce, conduct in church, relation to pagan religious practices, and charismatic gifts like "speaking in tongues." The two most important chapters are about Christian love (1 Cor 13) and the resurrection (1 Cor 15). Chapter 13 is probably the most famous chapter in the Bible.

Second Corinthians shows that many of the problems had not been solved. (Christians were not all models of wisdom and holiness then any more than now.) This letter is very personal and very emotional—more like a father talking to his problem children than like a theology professor to his students.

Galatians, like *Romans*, is about salvation by faith. The Galatians so missed this central point that Paul called their heresy of self-salvation "another gospel," that is, another religion, not Christianity. They thought they were saved by the law, that the way to Heaven was obeying the Ten Commandments, rather than faith in the one who said, "I am the way, the truth, and the life. No one can come to the Father but through Me." Many religiously uneducated Catholics still believe this Galatian heresy today. They desperately need to read *Galatians.*

After reading *Galatians*, they should read *James* to get "the rest of the story," as Paul Harvey would say. Though *James* doesn't come next in the Bible, I put it here because *James* is a very practical letter. Its basic point is that "faith without works is dead," it is not real faith. It will not save you. Faith and good works are like the root and flower of the same plant.

Ephesians is the Bible's greatest book about the Church as the Body of Christ. It is a deep and exalted meditation on the mystery of God's plan to save all men and women through Christ.

Philippians is full of personal intimacy, love, confidence, and joy (the word is used fourteen times in four pages). It contains some famous, eloquent, moving, and unforgettable passages (2:1-11, 3:4-14 and 4:8).

Colossians centers on how enormous Christ is (1:13-20) and how enormously he transforms our lives (3:1-17).

First Thessalonians is similar to *Colossians.* It contains a famous passage about Christ's Second Coming (5:1-11) that the Thessalonians misinterpreted. They left their jobs and sat around waiting for the end of the world! So Paul corrected their mistake in his second letter to them (2:1-17). Both letters are pastoral, personal, and practical.

First and *Second Timothy* were written to Paul's spiritual son or "junior apostle." Paul gives Timothy kindly, fatherly advice about how to be a good apostle, bishop, pastor, and preacher. *Titus* is written to another bishop about the same practical issues: doctrinal teaching, moral living, and church organization—the three visible aspects of religion ("words, works, and worship"). The two letters contain basic practical principles for the Church today as well as then.

Paul wrote the letter to Philemon to persuade him to receive back Onesimus, a runaway slave who had fled to Paul, "no longer as a slave but as a beloved brother." It is a little psychological masterpiece of reconciliation.

Hebrews (author unknown) is a systematic treatise on Christianity and Judaism, about how the new covenant (testament) fulfills and surpasses the old, about the superiority of Christ to Moses and the Jewish Levitical priesthood. Chapter 11, on the heroes of the faith, and chapter 12, on endurance in troubles, are especially eloquent.

Peter, the apostles' leader and the Church's first pope,

wrote his first letter to encourage Christians who were suffering persecution. Like James's letter, Peter's is very practical and ethical. His second letter warns against false and immoral teachers. It speaks of Christ's Second Coming and the end of the world.

First John is one of the most beautiful and "upbeat" letters ever written. It is graceful, poetic, elegant. "Light," "life," and "love" are its three main concepts. John's second and third letters, each less than a page long, warn against false teachers in the Church (again), as does the one-page letter of Jude.

The epistles are all about issues that are still with us today. Every one of them is utterly up-to-date. The Church's problems and God's solutions are essentially the same today as nineteen hundred years ago. The epistles are a major part of the Church's treasure-trove of wisdom for dealing with today's issues. They are like letters you find written many years ago by your mother, who is still alive and still teaching you her wisdom. Guided by Jesus and the Spirit, the wisdom of holy Mother Church never dies and is never out of date.

TEN

The First Systematic Christian Theology: Romans

S AMUEL TAYLOR COLERIDGE CALLED *Romans* "the most profound book in existence." Godet called it "the cathedral of the Christian faith." It is placed first among the epistles not only because it is the longest, but also because it is the greatest.

Romans was probably written shortly before Nero's persecution began in A.D. 64. According to Tacitus, the Roman historian, Christians were already "an immense multitude" then.

Paul had not founded the Roman church, Peter had. But Paul came to Rome to appear before the emperor and to be martyred. *Acts* ends with him preaching the Gospel from house arrest in Rome.

Rome was, of course, the center of the entire world, the greatest city in the world in power and population, but already decadent with slavery, political corruption, and extremes of wealth and poverty. Into this cesspool, Paul drops the seed of the Gospel, which was to conquer the world.

Romans is the only systematic theology in the Bible, except for *Hebrews*, which is not about Christianity as such but about Christianity and Judaism, like *Romans* 9-11. But Christianity is not a theory, a philosophy, but a story, "news." The epistles interpret this "news." They teach timeless truths, but truths about time: (1) the significance of the temporal events in the Gospels, especially Christ's death, the event each Gospel lingers longest over; and (2) the outworking of these events in our lifetimes.

The main point of *Romans*, as of Christianity, as of life itself, is Christ. *Romans* presents him as the Second Adam, the new man, and humanity's second chance. He is "the righteousness of God." This is the phrase Paul uses to identify his main theme at the beginning (1:16-17): "For I am not ashamed of the gospel; it is the power of God for salvation to every one who has faith, to the Jew first and also to the Greek. For in it the righteousness of God is revealed through faith for faith; as it is written, 'He who through faith is righteous shall live.'" This is a two-verse summary of the entire book.

Romans is the book that sparked the Protestant Reformation when Luther discovered the doctrine of justification by faith in it. The Catholic Church teaches this doctrine too, of course. The Church cannot contradict the Bible. That would be like a house contradicting its foundation. Nor is there any contradiction between Paul's doctrine of justification by faith (in *Romans* and *Galatians*) and James' teaching that faith without works is dead (Jas 2:14-26). Luther thought there was, and called *James* "an epistle of straw." But even *Romans* includes James' point. It ends with chapters 12-16 about the necessity of good works.

There is no book in the Bible in which it is more necessary to look at the outline. For *Romans* is an extended logical argument, especially chapters 1-8. The more you read, study, and think about it, the tighter and clearer it becomes. It is much better to do the detailed outlining yourself than to let any commentator do it for you. It may sound like dull "schoolwork," but I have found it extremely rewarding and even exciting.

The unity of the argument centers around four key concepts: *righteousness, faith, law,* and *sin.* Paul uses each term over sixty times. The main outline is as follows:

Personal Introduction: 1:1-15
Main Theme: 1:16-17
I. Doctrine
    A. Christianity
        1. The problem, the bad news, sin: 1:18-3:20
        2. The solution, the good news, salvation: 3:21-8:39
    B. Judaism: 9-11
II. Practice: 12-15
Personal postscripts: 16

At each major transition point in Paul's argument, there is a key "therefore" or "but."

The major transition, from sin to salvation, in the passage of 3:20-21, is this: "For no human being will be justified in his sight by works of the law... *But now* the righteousness of God has been manifested apart from law..." (emphasis mine).

Chapter 5 draws a corollary with another "therefore": "Therefore, since we are justified by faith, we have peace with God through our Lord Jesus Christ."

Chapter 6 also begins with a "therefore": "What shall we say then [therefore]? Are we to continue in sin that grace may abound? By no means!"

Finally, chapter 8, Paul's great, triumphant conclusion, begins with the final "therefore": "There is therefore now no condemnation for those who are in Christ Jesus." Each chapter expands upon its first verse, exploring a new step in the argument.

The first step is the problem, the "bad news" that we all have a mortal disease called sin, "The Jew first and also the Greek (Gentile)." The good news is that all are offered salvation, "The Jew first and also the Greek. For all have sinned and come short of the glory of God."

Gentiles may think they have an excuse because they

do not have divine revelation. So Paul first shows that Gentiles are inexcusable and responsible for their sins because they too know God, by nature and conscience. This passage (1:18-31) lays the foundation for "natural (rational) theology."

Jews may think they need no Savior because they do have revelation and are God's chosen people. Paul replies that the Jewish law cannot save you if you disobey it, and all do (2:1-3:8).

This demolishes the answer most Catholics give to the most important question in the world: how are you going to get to Heaven? Most Catholic students I have polled think they will be saved by their obedience to some law, whether the Ten Commandments or the principles of pop psychology.

The good news makes no sense unless you believe the bad news first. A free operation is not good news if you don't think you have a mortal disease. In a more realistic age, the main obstacle to believing in Christianity was the *good* news. It seemed like a fairy tale, too good to be true. Today the main obstacle is the *bad* news: people just don't believe in sin, even though that's the only Christian doctrine that can be proven simply by reading daily newspapers. When did you last hear anyone, even your priest, use "the s-word"?

Calling a person sinful is not to deny that his *being* remains good, any more than calling the statue of Venus de Milo a damaged work of art means denying that its sculptor created a masterpiece. Humanity is a good thing gone bad, the image of God in rebellion against God, God's beloved in a state of divorce.

The transition from the bad news (1:18-3:20) to the good news (3:21 ff.) is objectively Jesus' death and subjectively our faith. More exactly, Paul mentions three aspects of justification: by grace, by blood, and by faith. Its origin is grace (3:21-24), its means is Christ's death (3:25-26), and our reception of it is by faith (3:27-31).

Alternatively, the steps Paul distinguishes in God's plan for our salvation are: (1) the Father's plan and predestination,

(2) our justification by the death of the Son, and (3) our sanctification now and glorification hereafter by the Spirit. Salvation, like God, is trinitarian: and woe to any Christian— Lutheran or Catholic—who separates what God has joined together.

Chapter 4 proves that even Abraham was justified by faith. It incidentally demolishes the common fallacy that Judaism is only a religion of law, justice, judgment, and fear, while Christianity invented grace, mercy, forgiveness, and love.

Chapter 5 explores the *consequences* of justification by faith, including peace with God (5:1), joy in suffering (5:3-8), and hope rather than fear toward God's judgment (5:9-11).

Then comes the famous contrast between Adam and Christ (Second Adam), as the historical basis for the two main points, original sin and salvation.

Chapter 6 answers the natural objection: Why not go ahead and sin if we're saved by grace, not by law? The answer is that our identity is now bound up with Christ, we are new creatures, little Christs in a certain sense. We hate and avoid sin now not out of fear of punishment (the former motive), nor simply out of gratitude (Luther's answer, but not Paul's here), but because of *who we are:* Christ's. The point in *Romans* 6:1-3 is the same as in *1 Corinthians* 6:15.

If we are alive with Christ's life, we are dead to Adam, sin, and the law. Chapter 7 explores this death. God gave us the law not to save us but to reveal our sinfulness, not as our operation but as our X-ray. Not law but Spirit saves us—that is, God the Holy Spirit, really present in the believer's soul.

This salvation is completed by our sanctification. Jesus is called "Savior" not because he saves us only from *punishment* for sin but because he saves us from *sin.* The three trinitarian aspects of salvation are like the root, stem, and flower of a beautiful plant. But the flower is the fairest and the consummation. It is fitting, then, that chapter 8 is the fairest, most joyful chapter in the Bible. Our sanctification in this life (8:1-17) and our glorification in the next (8:18-39) are the point of the whole divine plot. Tolkien calls this "happy ending" the "eucatastrophe," the good catastrophe. "There is no tale ever told that men more wish to be true," he says. But unlike the lesser fairy tales, this one *is!*

The next three chapters in *Romans* show how Christianity views Judaism: their past election by God (ch. 9), their present rejection of God (ch. 10), and their future restoration by God (ch. 11).

The concluding practical, moral chapters include the seminal passage about the Christian and politics (13:1-7), love as the fulfillment of the law (13:10), the best passage in the Bible for the aging (13:11-12), the passage that delivered St. Augustine (13:14; see *Confessions* 8,12), and the meaning of "life or death" (14:7-8), among other gems. *Romans*, quite literally, shows us the way to Heaven, the way to receive God's greatest gift—eternal life with him. Who could ask for anything more or settle for anything less?

ELEVEN

How a Christian Is Different: First Corinthians

TODAY, ESPECIALLY IN AMERICA, Catholics, like everyone else (except Orthodox Jews and fundamentalists), want to be "accepted." Paul's *First Letter to the Corinthians* is especially relevant to such people. Though it talks about dozens of separate issues, the most unifying theme is that Christians must be different—the thing we don't dare to be today.

Corinth was the largest, most cosmopolitan, and most decadent city in Greece. Two-thirds of its seven hundred thousand citizens were slaves. It was a major port and hub of commerce. Much of the commerce was in human flesh. "To act like a Corinthian" was an ancient saying meaning debauchery, especially prostitution. Men went to Corinth to take a moral holiday.

The city was also full of idolatry, which centered around Aphrodite, the goddess of sex. Her temple, atop a eighteen-hundred-foot promontory, had a thousand temple prostitutes. Paul had come here in the years A.D. 51 and 52 to evangelize. Now four or five years later, he writes this letter to address some of the problems of this new, struggling Church surrounded by an "advanced" world just like ours: a world in "advanced" stages of decay.

His main point is that Christians are called out of paganism to a radically distinctive lifestyle. For Christ is the Lord of every aspect of life. Paul is utterly Christocentric; in *1 Corinthians* 1:30 he identifies four great abstract ideals (wisdom, righteousness, sanctification, and redemption) with Christ himself. In *1 Corinthians* 2:2 he says that he "decided to know nothing among you except Jesus Christ." Any addition to *him* would be a subtraction.

America is strikingly similar to Corinth. According to polls, most Catholics consider themselves "Americans who happen to be Catholics," rather than "Catholics who happen to be Americans." Two of the words they dislike the most are "authority" (or "lordship") and "obedience." Yet these are precisely what Paul calls for.

Christ always sought out the most needy, and his Church has always followed his lead. Christianity naturally flows to the lowest places, like water. Corinth was the world's lowest place, the spiritual gutter. Yet the Corinthians thought of themselves as high, not low—like the high and airy Temple of Aphrodite. For one thing, they were rich due to trade and prostitution. For another, they were well educated. Though they did not produce any philosophers, many philosophers from Athens taught there. The most prominent philosophical school at the time was probably Skepticism. The last thing any of them would believe was a man rising from the dead.

Into this atmosphere heavy with lust, greed, and pride, Paul had introduced the clear light of Jesus when he first visited (2:1-5). And he now continues the same strategy: not compromising, not pandering, not patronizing, but calling for the hard way, the distinctive way of living the life of Christ in a Christless world.

This is not a systematically ordered letter, like *Romans*. It moves from topic to topic. There are many minor topics, but the four major ones are (1) sectarianism, (2) faith and reason—Christianity and philosophy, (3) sex and love, and (4) the resurrection from the dead—both Christ's and ours. Other topics include incest, pagan lawyers, eating food offered to idols, prostitution, virginity, marriage, divorce, the Eucharist, order in worship, speaking in tongues, and other spiritual gifts.

The first two of these major points are treated together since simple faith unites while pride in reason divides. Paul is utterly scandalized at the embryonic factionalism in the Corinthian church (1:10-13). Can anyone seriously wonder which of the many "denominations" he would approve today?

Paul sees the source of division as the proud claim to possess superior "wisdom" and not submitting to Christ as God's wisdom. The wonderful irony and paradox of God's folly being wiser than human wisdom (1:18-3:23) is the definitive passage for philosophers or theologians with "original" minds who tend to resist Christocentrism and want to "advance" in different and schismatic directions.

If all Christians had kept this passage uppermost in their minds for the last two thousand years, I believe that the tragedies of 1054 and 1517 and the hundreds of tears in the seamless garment of the Church since then could never have happened. If the Church ever becomes visibly one again, this passage will be the foundation for unity, although she always remains substantially and invisibly one, holy, Catholic, and apostolic.

On the number one topic in modern morality, sex and love, Paul does three things. First, he condemns sexual immorality in chapters 5 and 6, and the Corinthians' lax attitudes that accepted it. Instead of justifying incest, they should excommunicate the offender. Instead of justifying prostitution by the slogan "all things are lawful" (6:12), they should realize that a Christian, as a member of Christ's body, makes *Christ* fornicate with a prostitute (6:15)!

Second, Paul gives a positive alternative picture of Christian marriage in chapter 7. Here he clearly distinguishes God's commands from his own opinion, which is to stay single. I think there is a wonderful divine humor in God revealing some deep and perennial principles of marriage through a celibate who confesses that he personally does not recommend it! I also see a wry divine humor in including in Scripture (7:6-12) a clear distinction between what is divine revelation and what is not. The distinction between divine revelation and human opinion is included within divine revelation, not human opinion!

Third, Paul writes the most famous passage about love ever written, chapter 13. This is the essential alternative to pagan lust for both married and unmarried. It is also a call to a clear and distinctive lifestyle and Christian witness. After all, Christ had prophesied that the world would be able to distinguish Christians from others by the special kind of love they had (Jn 13:35), not by having the same kind of love as the world had.

First Corinthians 13 is often read at weddings because it is the best definition of love ever written. This love (*agape*) is not a feeling or desire (*eros*) but a *life;* it is as Dostoyevski put it, "love in action" rather than "love in dreams."

The first paragraph (13:1-3) shows the infinite value of love by contrasting it with other things of great value: speaking in tongues, prophecy, knowledge, faith, and even the works of love without the soul of love.

The second paragraph distinguishes this love from all others by describing it in fifteen characteristics (vv. 4-7). Love is the skeleton key that unlocks all these doors. For instance, it is impossible to be patient with difficult people without love, but love brings patience with it.

Finally, the last paragraph shows the eternal destiny of love. Everything else, including all the things the Corinthians set their hearts and lives on, is doomed to die. Even faith and hope and earthly wisdom are not needed after death. But love is. When we love now, we plant seeds for eternity.

Chapter 13 is sandwiched between two chapters on spiritual gifts, especially the gift of tongues, and their use in worship. Paul shows moderation and wisdom in avoiding both the extremes of enthusiasm and suspicion, and in subordinating everything, even supernatural gifts, to love. He himself speaks in tongues and wants everyone to (14:5,18) but the issue is much less important for Paul than most charismatics *and* other Christians think.

Next to chapter 13, chapter 15 is the most famous and most important. It is the primary text in Scripture on the resurrection of the body. None of the Greek philosophers in Corinth believed in bodily resurrection, not because they did not believe in miracles, but because they did not believe the body was good and created by God. Their sexual materialism and their philosophical spiritualism went hand in hand. Paul revealed instead that the body is more real and good and important than they thought. It is a holy thing, the Spirit's temple now (6:19) and the seed of something destined to live with God eternally, not a mere animal organism seeking sexual pleasure as its greatest good.

Plato had called the body "the soul's tomb." Paul tells the Corinthians, who were probably influenced by this philosophy, that to deny or ignore Christ's bodily resurrection is to abandon the whole faith. Without the resurrection, "our preaching is in vain, and your faith is in vain" (15:14), "you are still in your sins" (15:17), and "if for this life only we have hoped in Christ, we are of all men most to be pitied" (15:19).

And this resurrection is no mere symbol, no merely subjective and spiritual "resurrection of Easter faith," or some such silly subterfuge. The Greek words for "the resurrection of the body" are *anastasis nekron,* which means "the sitting-up of the corpse!" Denial of the literal resurrection, according to the Word of God, is denial of Christ, of the faith.

After demonstrating its existence (15:12-34), Paul gives some hints about its nature (15:35-58) through natural analogies. This body is the seed of another one. This body is as different from the resurrection body as a planet differs from a star. Paul's contrast between a "physical body" and a "spiritual body" does not mean that the post-resurrection body will not be tangible. Christ's was and is. It means that the source of this physical body is *physis,* nature, the dust we return to, while the source of our resurrection body is the Spirit of God, who will raise us as he raised Christ.

Paul concludes the great chapter with words that sound like trumpets (indeed, that is why Handel accompanied them with a trumpet in his "Messiah"). He concludes by sticking his tongue out at death, taunting it: "O death, where is thy victory? O death, where is thy sting?" Death is a stingless bee because its stinger is in the body of Christ crucified. He took the stinger of Hell out of the bee of death for us.

The central theme in each of the specific topics Paul deals with (probably from questions in a letter the Corinthians had written to him) is the theme of Christian distinctiveness. This is seen most strikingly in chapter 6, where Paul is scandalized that Christians sue other Christians before pagan lawyers and judges. No one today even blinks at that practice, for we have so radically lost that sense of distinctiveness. But why would a cat go before a dog to adjudicate a dispute with another cat? The difference between a Christian and a non-Christian is like the difference between a cat and a dog. It is not, to Paul, a difference between two *beliefs* merely, but a difference between two *beings,* two species.

I continually ask my theology and philosophy classes the simple question, "According to the New Testament, what is a Christian?" They always answer it not according to the New Testament but according to something else. For they always say what a Christian thinks, or believes, or feels, or does, or likes, or desires, but not what a Christian *is.* Paul knew what a Christian is: a Christian is a little Christ, a member of Christ, a cell in Christ's body.

From this radical transformation everything else is transformed. As he was to put it in his second letter to these Corinthians (5:17), "If any one is in Christ, he is a new creation." In our desperate, bored search for novelties and "new theologies," we can never be more radically new than to simply rest on "the Church's one foundation—Jesus Christ her Lord."

TWELVE

A Different Christ Means No Christ: Second Corinthians

T HIS IS THE MOST INTENSELY PERSONAL, passionate and intimate of all Paul's letters. Though there is not as much
doctrinal or moral teaching content here as in his other letters, there is more emotion, personal confession, biographi-
cal revelation, and direct personal address.

Between the time Paul wrote his first letter to the Corinthians and the time of this second letter, false teachers had
turned the Corinthian Christians against him. They were
probably reacting against the strong principles and discipline
in the first letter, just as all "dissenters" from Church doctrine today want to minimize, not maximize; weaken, not
strengthen; subtract, not add to, the fullness and power of the
principles of the Gospel.

These false teachers denied Paul's authority as an apostle
(11:5) and preached "another Jesus," another religion,
another Gospel. Paul's response is passionate not because his
authority has been challenged but because the authority of
Christ has. He responds in words few would dare to use today
in similar situations. For a different Christ means no Christ,
no Savior, and no salvation. Only in *Galatians* (1:8) did Paul
respond so strongly, for the same reason.

Paul made a quick trip to Corinth to settle the controversy before he wrote this letter, but he was unsuccessful. Pained and humiliated, he wrote a troubled letter to the Corinthians between the time of the two letters we have. This is mentioned in 2:3-4 and 7:8-12. Some scholars think this letter was preserved and put into *2 Corinthians*, as chapters 10-13, because the sarcasm of these chapters is in such strong contrast to the joy and tenderness of chapters 1-9. But this argument ignores the fact that parents and lovers are often moved by passion and intimacy to both tenderness and despair almost simultaneously.

The content theme of *2 Corinthians* is the distinctiveness of the Christian, the Christian's faith, and the Christian's life in an unbelieving world. This was the theme of *1 Corinthians* also. As medieval Christendom recedes more and more and paganism returns more and more, these two letters become more and more directly relevant to our lives. Paul's essential insight here is close to that of *Colossians*: the supreme importance and total lordship of Christ in the Christian's life; for "if any one is in Christ, he is a new creation; the old has passed away, behold, the new has come" (5:17).

Two of the distinctive highlights of this letter are (1) the only account in the New Testament of a mystical experience: Paul's own (12:1-10). It is striking that he recounts this only to relegate it to a second, lower place compared to his weakness and suffering—a much more effective means to sanctity. Also (2) the most complete and lengthy passage in the Bible about generosity or Christian giving (ch.s 8 and 9) is in this letter.

Other familiar, eloquent passages are 3:17, 3:18, 4:7, 4:10, 4:16-18, 5:6-7, 5:21, 6:2, 6:8-10, 8:9, and 10:5. Paul could never write a letter without writing unforgettable quotes.

In *1 Corinthians*, Paul is on top of the problems of his beloved "problem children" in Corinth. In *2 Corinthians*, he is wrung out and even exasperated. Like Christ, Paul experienced all natural human emotions. I think God must feel exactly the same toward us, *his* "problem children."

THIRTEEN

Back to Basics: Galatians

GALATIANS IS THE ONLY LETTER OF PAUL'S that does not contain a single word of praise. Even when Paul wrote to the Corinthians, who were having *very* serious problems, including getting drunk at the Eucharist, practicing and justifying incest and prostitution, splitting the church into rival factions, arrogance and superiority about the gift of tongues, and proudly placing pagan philosophy above the Christian faith—even when he wrote to a church with all these shocking problems, Paul still found something to praise them for and to thank God for in them (1 Cor 1:4-7). Not so at Galatia. Instead of the customary praise, he begins with this sledgehammer paragraph:

"I am astonished that you are so quickly deserting him who called you in the grace of Christ and turning to a different gospel—not that there is another gospel, but there are some who trouble you and want to pervert the gospel of Christ. But even if we, or an angel from heaven, should preach to you a gospel contrary to that which we preached to you, let him be accursed" (1:6-8).

What elicited such Pauline heat and outrage? The mistakes of the Corinthians were mistakes of addition; the mistake of the Galatians was subtraction. The Corinthians had polluted the Gospel. The Galatians had abandoned it for another religion, "a different gospel." No mistake could be more serious. Yet as we shall see, this is the single most common mistake in the Church *today*.

Another way of seeing how crucial the issue is, is to notice that Paul feels he has to begin his letter by "pulling rank" and establishing his authority as an apostle, equal to the eleven and Peter (1:11-2:14). The Galatians may not listen to argument, but Paul hopes that they will at least listen to authority.

An immediate and specific issue masked the more fundamental one. The immediate issue was whether Christians had to be circumcised. The more fundamental one was how to be saved. The first issue is a total non-issue today; *no* Christians think it is necessary to be circumcised. But the second issue, alas, is still very much at issue. It was the issue that split the Church in the Protestant Reformation. And if the informal questions and formal questionnaires that I give to my college students are any indication, not a small minority but a large majority of Catholics today not only do not know the basic doctrines of Catholic theology any more, they do not even know how to get to Heaven!

Until this unbelievable failure is remedied, it is pointless to pray to God for ecumenical peace and reunion between Christian churches. For ecumenical unity means unity among *Christians,* and it is not clear that one who does not even know how to get to Heaven can accurately be called a Christian.

I am not suggesting, as many Protestant fundamentalists do, that most Catholics are not saved. But I am suggesting that perhaps most will be saved as good pagans, as "anonymous Christians" rather than as Catholic Christians. For when the time comes to present their entrance ticket for the heavenly plane (God has a large angel air force: see Mk 13:27), if they do not present Christ as their Savior, but only present themselves as "good people," can this be called Christianity? If the responses I hear are typical, many will rely instead on the same old "other gospel" the Galatians relied on, namely, the works of law, or more likely on the updated, "soft" revision of it, good *intentions.* "I'm a good person," "I try to do good," "I'm sincere," and "I try not to hurt people" are four of the most common counterfeit tickets I see. They all begin with the same fatal word.

What *I* say about this matters nothing. But let's see what God's apostle says about this. He says, in effect, that whatever the answer I give at the gate of Heaven it had better not begin with my favorite word, "I", but with the Word, Christ. The Word had better be my favorite word.

The connection between circumcision and salvation is this: the point of being circumcised, in Old Testament Judaism, was like the point of being baptized in Catholicism: you thus enter a new community of faith and a covenant with God. You bind yourself to the covenant, bind yourself to obey its laws, just as you do when you get married (the marriage "covenant"). Thus, being circumcised—the immediate issue in Galatia—meant relying on the law for salvation. This is the fundamental issue.

There was also a third intermediate issue *between* circumcision and salvation: Judaism. Being circumcised meant becoming a Jew. Must one become a Jew before becoming a Christian? Those in Galatia who were insisting on circumcision were making Christianity a Jewish sect, forgetting the radical break between the two religions, namely that Christ was the stone of stumbling and the rock of offense. According to Christianity, we are saved *not* by the Jewish law, the old covenant, entered by circumcision. We are saved by Christ and by his new covenant, entered by faith.

Paul points out very simply and clearly that no one can be saved by the law: "We... know that a man is not justified [saved] by the works of the law but through faith in Jesus Christ... because by works of the law shall no one be justified" (2:15-16; see 3:11). The simple reason why no one can be saved by obeying God's law is that no one obeys it! (Is 64:6; Phil 3:9).

If we were saved by obeying the law, we would save our-selves and would not need a savior. Jesus would then be reduced to a human teacher, prophet, guru, social worker, psychologist, philosopher, or moral example—as in much modernist theology.

The law is like an X-ray. Sin is like cancer. Salvation is like an operation. Jesus is like the surgeon. Faith is like consent to the operation. The Galatian heresy is thinking the X-ray will save you.

Salvation occurs by faith alone (though, as we shall see in the last half of Paul's letter, it is completed by good works) because faith is not just some subjective process inside our psyches, but an objective transaction: *believing* means *receiving* (Jn 1:12).

Thus Paul contrasts law and faith (2:16; 3:11; see Eph 2:8-10) as candidates for the answer to the most important question anyone can ask: "What must I do to be saved?" (Acts 16:30). The point is so crucial—how could anything possibly be more important than eternity?—that Paul equates turning away from this doctrine with turning away from Christ (1:6). He even calls the Galatians fools under the spell of witchcraft (3:1) for abandoning it.

Paul uses five lines of argument to prove his main point.

First, this Gospel "is not man's gospel. For I did not receive it from man... but... through a revelation of Jesus Christ" (1:11-12). When Paul submitted this teaching to the apostles in Jerusalem, they all acknowledged its truth and authority (2:1-10). Paul even rightly corrected Peter when he failed to apply it (2:11-21). On the basis of the doctrine he also accepted, Peter failed to live it out when he submitted to Jewish laws only when he was with Jews (2:11-16). Paul's dis-pute with a pope was like that of St. Teresa of Avila: not with the teaching but with the failure to live the teaching.

Second, Paul argues that men and women are saved by faith, not by the law, even in Old Testament times. This is shown in the case of Abraham, who received the promise *before* Moses received the law. Paul uses the same argument in *Galatians* 3 as in *Romans* 4.

Third, the purpose of the law cannot be to save because its purpose is to condemn, to specify sins (3:19-22). It is the diagnosis, not the cure; the bad news, not the good news.

Fourth, the law is essentially preparatory. It is like a custodian or child's nurse (3:23-26), who takes the child to school but does not teach him—like the school bus driver. Slaves are under law. Family heirs are under promise, and we are family heirs by adoption (4:1-7), not servants but sons and daughters of God.

Fifth, the law binds us while the Gospel frees us (4:8-31). Thus the two are opposed, not identical. Paul illustrates this by allegorizing Abraham's two rival sons, Isaac (faith) and Ishmael (law) (4:22-31).

So far, Paul sounds like a Protestant evangelist. But in chapters 5 and 6 he sounds like a Catholic moralist. He is both, of course; for the Gospel transforms morality as well as salvation.

Paul admitted that the law *defined* sins (3:19-22), but the law does not *save* us from either sin or sin's punishment. God's grace, received by faith, does both. Not only justification (being made right with God) but also sanctification (being made holy) have the Spirit, not the law, as their source and power. ("Spirit" means not man's spirit but the Holy Spirit here.) Christians cannot be legalists because they have been freed from the law by Christ. They are now no longer under the law but under grace.

But *license* is as far from Christianity as *legalism*. In fact, these two apparent opposites are two sides of the same coin. Both rely on self, not God. Neither can say, "I have been crucified with Christ; *it is no longer I who live, but Christ who lives in me;* and the life I now live in the flesh I live by faith in the Son of God, who loved me and gave himself for me" (2:20 emphasis mine). *That* is the good news; that is the thing both opposite heresies miss; that is the link between faith and works, between justification and sanctification, between being saved and being virtuous. The life of Christ comes into the soul by faith and out by works. It is not that you get to Heaven because you live a good life. Rather, you live a good life because Heaven has gotten to you.

Legalism, license, and liberty are three totally opposite ways of life, three different religions, and three different kinds of love. Legalism is self-love and self-righteousness. License is self-love and self-indulgence. Liberty is selfless love of God and neighbor: "No longer I... but Christ in me."

Paul concludes *Galatians* by talking about virtue and good works because that is part of the Gospel too. Works as well as faith are part of salvation, just as fruit as well as roots are part of a tree. If we have no good works, we are not saved, for faith without works is dead faith, fake faith (Jas 2:14-26). Luther could not see this, and dismissed *James* as an "epistle of straw." That's because he didn't see the living link between faith and works. That link is the very life of Christ in the soul which gives us a second, divine nature (2 Pt 1:4), a new birth (Jn 3:3-6).

Luther could not see this essential theological truth because bad philosophy held him back. Bad philosophy can produce bad theology. Luther was an Ockhamist, that is, a Nominalist, who did not believe there were any such things as real species or universal essences like human nature. If there is no real universal human nature, there can be no second nature or transformed nature.

Luther thus reduced salvation to a mental attitude on God's part (God *looks* at us *as if* we were his children because he looks at us covered by Christ's blood which hides our sins) and to a legal transaction (God *declares* us righteous even though we really aren't). This merely transfers the legalism from the human to the divine. Catholic theology more perfectly fulfills Luther's own desire to escape legalism than Lutheran theology does.

Paul ends by contrasting the two kinds of life, *bios* and *zoe*, natural and supernatural, "flesh" and "spirit." "Flesh" (*sarx*) and "spirit" (*pneuma*) do not mean body (*soma*) and soul (*psyche*) but (1) fallen human nature inherited from Adam and (2) the very life of God the Holy Spirit given by Christ. "The works of the flesh" listed in 5:19-21 include both mental and physical sins. "The fruit of the Spirit" listed in 5:22-23 include both corporal and spiritual virtues.

Galatians is Paul's simplest letter. Once you see its single central point, you see how everything he says is a spoke in the single wheel that is held together by that hub. Once you know that hub, you know what Christianity essentially is: Christ himself (Col 1:27-28). Without a firm grasp of that center, heresies are bound to come, whether legalistic or licentious. "This is the true God and eternal life. Little children, keep yourselves from idols" (1 Jn 5:20-21).

FOURTEEN

We Are Christ's Mystical Body: Ephesians

E *PHESIANS* IS TO THE EPISTLES what *John's Gospel* is to the Gospels: the most mystical, profound, and universal of them all.

Paul probably wrote *Ephesians, Philippians, Colossians,* and *Philemon* from prison in Rome around A.D. 60 or 62. *Ephesians* seems to be an encyclical (circulating) letter for all the churches in the region (Asia Minor), for it mentions no specific problems or controversies in any local church. Its topic is universal—totally universal, in fact. We may call it Paul's treatise on "the cosmic Christ."

Ephesians, like life, is really only about one thing: Christ. But we can distinguish at least twelve sub-themes or aspects of this single point.

1. The mystery of *predestination*—that God "chose us in him [Christ] before the foundation of the world" (1:4) and "destined us in love to be his sons through Jesus Christ" (1:5)—implies a Christian philosophy of history in which Christ makes a *total* difference. The Christian era is the fulfillment of this divine "plan for the fulness of time, to unite all things in him [Christ]" (1:10).

2. *How big* is this Christ? Colossal, as *Colossians* will point out (Col 1:15-20; 2:3,7), gigantic, cosmic, even more than

cosmic. For Christ is "far above all rule and authority and power and domination, and above every name that is named, not only in this age but in that which is to come... he has put all things under his feet" (1:21-22).

The classic passage about the "length and breadth and depth and height" of Christ is *Ephesians* 3:14-21. I think it is the second most exalted passage in Scripture, next to *Romans* 8:31-39. If you are wise, you will stop reading this chapter and read that passage right now, slowly and prayerfully.

3. *Christian wisdom* means perceiving the size, the all-inclusiveness, of Christ. Paul writes this letter for that purpose: "that the God of our Lord Jesus Christ... may give you a spirit of wisdom and of revelation in the knowledge of him, having the eyes of your hearts enlightened, that you may know... what are the riches of his glorious inheritance in the saints, and what is the immeasurable greatness of his power in us who believe" (1:17-19). In the words of an old classic title by J.B. Phillips, Paul's message to the Ephesians (and to us) is that "Your God Is Too Small."

4. A theme that could well be called the central theme of *Ephesians* is *the Church as Christ's Mystical Body,* an invisble organism, not just visible organization. *Ephesians* has been the basis of much of the Church's theology of herself ever since Pope Pius XII's great landmark encyclical "The Mystical Body of Christ."

Paul calls the Church "his body, the fulness of him who fills all in all" (1:23). Therefore the Church "fills all in all." As G.K. Chesterton says, the Church is not in the world, the world is in the Church, as a setting is in a play. God created the universe for the Church, for his Son's body, for his family.

And we are actually, literally, parts or organs of Christ's body. Paul uses the metaphor of a living building, "Christ Jesus himself being the cornerstone, in whom the whole structure is joined together and grows into a holy temple in the Lord, in whom you also are built into it..." (2:20-22). The building is only a metaphor, but the body is not.

5. In this body, *Jews and Gentiles* are united (2:11-21). Gentiles, who were "separated from Christ, alienated from the commonwealth of Israel" (2:12) are now "no longer strangers and sojourners but fellow citizens with the saints" (2:19). For in Christ God planned to "create in himself one new man [the whole Christ, head and body] in place of the two" (2:15). This is what Paul calls "the mystery of Christ" (3:4-6): his extension through the whole Gentile world.

By way of aside, Jews do not send out missionaries, for Orthodox Jews believe that only when the Messiah comes will the Gentiles be given the knowledge of the true God. It was Christians who fulfilled this Jewish prophecy. Secular Jews, of course, like secularized Christians, have no missionaries because they have no mission.

6. "The unsearchable *riches of Christ*... in whom we have boldness and confidence of access" to God (3:8,12) are infinite. Christians are like millionaires content to draw pennies from their account. Paul lists Christians' assets throughout the first half of *Ephesians.* The second half draws out the radical implications for living. There are no imperatives, no "oughts" in the first half—only facts. All are based on our being "in Christ"—a phrase Paul uses over thirty times in this short letter.

7. These infinite riches are *pure grace,* pure gift. *Ephesians* repeats the theme of *Romans* and *Galatians:* "For by grace you have been saved through faith; and this is not your own doing, it is the gift of God—not because of works, lest any man should boast. For we are his workmanship, created in Christ Jesus for good works, which God prepared beforehand, that we should walk in them" (2:8-10). Works are the fruit of faith, and as much a part of God's predestined plan for our salvation as faith. But the whole plan first comes as pure gift, simply received by faith.

8. What we have received is the most radical change conceivable: a new mind and *a new life.* "And you he made alive when you were dead through [your] trespasses and sins"

(2:1). Everything is different for a Christian, for Christianity is not just a new lifestyle, but a new life.

9. But we must *grow* into this new life "until we all attain to the unity of the faith and of the knowledge of the Son of God, to mature manhood, to the measure of the stature of the fulness of Christ" (4:13). "We are to grow up in every way into him who is the head, into Christ" (4:15). *That* is the definition of "maturity."

10. In this body we are "*members one of another*" (4:25) because we are members of Christ. "Members" here means not "members" of a *group*, like a political party or a social club, but members of a *body*, like ears and toes. As Pascal says, "imagine a body of thinking members."

This is the Christian basis for total truth and honesty: "... let everyone speak the truth with his neighbor, *for we are members one of another*" (4:25, emphasis mine). A far more powerful basis for "communication" than any human psychology.

11. In this body there are three main *relationships*. We find the same three relationships in all societies in the world, but in Christ they are all transformed. They are husband-wife, parent-child, and ruler-ruled (in Paul's world, that included master-slave).

Each of the two parties in each of these three relationships has reciprocal but diverse duties; there is neither one-way superiority and privilege nor dull, flat, repetitive equality. Each owes a different form of the same thing—love—to the other. In each case there are two things that the modern mind scorns: authority and obedience. But these are of a radically different kind in the Church than in the world. *Ephesians* 5 is really Paul's working out of the consequences of *Matthew* 20:25-28.

Wives, children, and slaves are liberated by Christ from inferiority. But they are told to obey, not to disobey. For their obedience is to be no longer that of the world, based on force and fear, but that of Christ, based on faith and love.

If you think it is demeaning to obey, consider who was the most obedient person in history: God incarnate. Christ obeyed his Father in all things (Jn 5:30; 6:38). If obedience is the mark of inferiority, Christ was the most inferior man who ever lived. See how far our minds are from being transformed? We still think with worldly categories if we shrink back from Christ's call for obedience to each other.

Ephesians 5:21-33 is the most profound passage in the Bible on the most fundamental institution in the world, the one whose decay is destroying our civilization: marriage. Christian marriage, says Paul, is not just a good thing, but a profound mystery that refers to Christ and the Church (5:32). There are three in every Christian marriage, not two, as Fulton Sheen put it in the title of his classic on marriage, *Three to Get Married.*

This is the key to interpreting the most hated and resented verse in Scripture today, *Ephesians* 5:22: "Wives, be subject to your husbands...." For Paul adds the phrase that transforms everything: "as to the Lord." In this Lord there is no lording it over, no chauvinism, no bossiness. Christ is not the "boss" of the Church, but its *head.* And "the husband is the head of the wife *as Christ is the head of the Church, his body*" (5:23, emphasis mine).

Christ is the "head" of the Church as the round thing between your shoulders is the head of your body, not as an executive is the head of his corporation. And only a neurotic head tries to enslave its own body. "Even so husbands should love their wives *as their own bodies....* For no man ever hates his own flesh" (5:28-29, emphasis mine). What we have here is a radical alternative to both the old chauvinism and the new egalitarianism. Here we have organic unity, ontological intimacy, the one flesh of head and body, a great mystery (5:32).

12. Though this new life in Christ is love and marriage, it is also war. *Spiritual warfare* is one of the most common themes in the lives of the saints, but it is almost totally neglected today. *Ephesians* 6:12-17 is Scripture's most famous passage about it.

Paul makes clear that this is *spiritual* warfare, not physical. "For we are not contending against flesh and blood, but against the principalities, against the powers, against the world rulers of this present darkness, against the spiritual hosts of wickedness in the heavenly places." We are, like it or not, wrestling against demons. Ignorance of this fact is as disastrous as an army's ignorance of an opposing army.

Since this is spiritual warfare, we have spiritual weapons, "the whole armor of God." This includes (1) the loincloth of truth, (2) the breastplate of righteousness, (3) the shoes of the Gospel, (4) the shield of faith, and (5) the sword of the Spirit, the Word of God (6:13-17; see Heb 4:12). In this war, "if God is for us, who can be against us?" (Rom 8:31). Goliath doesn't stand a chance against the Son of David, *and we are the body of the Son of David.* You don't read *Ephesians* aright unless it makes you want to shout, "Hallelujah!"

FIFTEEN

Christ-Mindedness: Philippians

PHILIPPIANS IS NEITHER A TREATISE on systematic theology, like *Romans*, nor a treatment of one point of it, like *Galatians*. Nor is it a practical, moral letter answering many specific questions and local problems, like *1 Corinthians*. It is a pastoral, personal, intimate letter whose unifying theme is *sanctity*, or Christ-mindedness (2:5). It was written from house arrest in Rome where Paul was awaiting death.

Along this broad unifying thread, Paul strings pearls: some of the most moving, memorable, and oft-quoted passages in all of Scripture. Since the structural outline is not prominent, the best way to introduce this little gem of a letter is to point out some of these passages, like a tour guide showing stunning highlights of a small exotic island.

1. The letter begins with a dash of confidence for parents, pastors, and those entrusted to care for souls in danger of losing the faith: "I am sure that he who began a good work in you will bring it to completion at the day of Jesus Christ" (1:6). For faith is a work of God, and God never gives up and never fails.

2. The whole Christian life is summed up in two words in the passage of 1:9-10: love and discernment. "It is my prayer that your love may abound more and more, with knowledge

and all discernment, so that you may approve what is excellent." All you need is love, but love needs eyes.

3. The most perfect and simple statement ever written of the meaning of life and of death is in the passage of 1:21: "For me to live is Christ, and to die is gain." In other words, death is only more Christ. Like Christ, Paul does not describe sanctity as *imitating* Christ but as living in Christ and living out Christ: "for me to live is Christ" (compare Jn 15:4-5). Denying the real presence of Christ in the Christian is as harmful a heresy as denying the real presence of Christ in the Eucharist. Just imagine: suppose we all *really* believed *Matthew* 25:40!

4. The most famous passage in *Philippians* is the "kenosis" passage (2:5-11), which demands of all Christians the same "emptying"as the incarnation: "Have this mind among yourselves, which is yours in Christ Jesus, who, though he was in the form of God, did not count equality with God a thing to be grasped, but emptied himself, taking the form of a servant, being born in the likeness of men. And being found in human form he humbled himself and became obedient unto death, even death on a cross."

Like Buddhism, Christianity is mercilessly threatening to the "grasping" greed and desire in which the world finds its hope for happiness. But unlike Buddhism, Christianity has a positive alternative. It does not call for an empty mind but a taking on of the mind of Christ and the hope of glory: "Therefore God has highly exalted him and bestowed on him the name which is above every name, that at the name of Jesus every knee should bow, in heaven and on earth and under the earth, and every tongue confess that Jesus Christ is Lord, to the glory of God the Father" (2:9-11).

5. In the life of the Christian, our free will and God's grace are one, as they were in the life of Christ. The mystery no philosopher can solve is stated in all its paradoxical force in the passage of 2:12-13: "… work out your own salvation with fear and trembling; for God is at work in you, both to

will and to work for his good pleasure."

6. A perfect slogan for the Christian in a decadent and dying culture, whether ancient Rome or modern America, is 2:15: "... be blameless and innocent, children of God without blemish in the midst of a crooked and perverse generation, among whom you shine as lights in the world...." Jesus told us the same thing: to be lights, to be salt, to be distinctive. God never told anyone to be popular, not even a bishop. God does not respect the American Zeitgeist.

7. With this advice goes another: to "glory in Christ Jesus, and put no confidence in the flesh" (3:3). Modern American Christians lack Christ's *realism*. Aren't we shocked by John 2:23-24? We remember that human nature is precious, but we forget that it is fallen. We remember to love human beings, but we forget to put our faith and hope in God, *not* in human beings. That's why our faith falters when we hear of clerical scandals.

8. Paul practices what he preaches. He himself puts no confidence in the flesh, that is, human and worldly advantages. After listing all his considerable advantages (3:4-8), he summarizes them in a shocking four-letter word which no Bible since the sixteenth century has dared to translate literally:

> If any other man thinks he has reason for confidence in the flesh, I have more: circumcised on the eighth day, of the people of Israel, of the tribe of Benjamin, a Hebrew born of Hebrews; as to the law a Pharisee, as to zeal, a persecutor of the church, as to the righteousness under the law blameless. But whatever gain I had, I counted as loss for the sake of Christ. Indeed I count everything as loss because of the surpassing worth of knowing Christ Jesus my Lord. For his sake I have suffered the loss of all things and count them as refuse.

"Refuse" (*skubala*) begins with an "s" in modern English.

Paul's point is not that the world is worthless, but that its very great worth is nothing compared with Christ. A trillion is nothing compared with infinity.

9. The goal of this life in Christ is summarized in unforgettable words in 3:10-11: "that I may know him and the power of his resurrection, and may share his sufferings, becoming like him in his death, that if possible I may attain the resurrection of the dead."

A constant incompleteness and energy animates the Christian life, like a race: "Not that I have already obtained this or am already perfect; but I press on to make it my own, because Christ Jesus has made me his own. Brethren, I do not consider that I have made it my own; but one thing I do, forgetting what lies behind and straining forward to what lies ahead, I press on toward the goal for the prize of the upward call of God in Christ Jesus" (3:12-14). Salvation is both complete—he said, "It is finished"—and incomplete. For while God has completely made us his own, we have not completely made him our own.

10. Christians who pin their hopes to a political or national agenda had better read 3:20-21, a definition of Christian patriotism and the Christian *patria* (fatherland): "Our commonwealth is in heaven, and from it we await a Savior, the Lord Jesus Christ, who will change our lowly body to be like his glorious body, by the power which enables him to subject all things to himself."

11. For the listless and despondent, Paul has a command —not just an "ideal"—to "rejoice in the Lord always; again I will say, rejoice" (4:4). It's worth repeating a few hundred times a day. Try it. See the difference it makes.

12. Perhaps the most beloved of all benedictions is 4:7: "And the peace of God, which passes all understanding, will keep your hearts and your minds in Christ Jesus." The peace that comes from understanding will keep the mind, but only the peace that surpasses understanding can keep the heart that surpasses the mind.

13. The perfect definition of Christ-mindedness comes in

4:8: "Finally, brethren, whatever is true, whatever is honorable, whatever is just, whatever is pure, whatever is lovely, whatever is gracious, if there is any excellence, if there is anything worthy of praise, think about these things."

Elsewhere (2 Cor 10:5) Paul commands us to "take every thought captive to obey Christ." For thought is the source of all life: "Sow a thought, reap an act; sow an act, reap a habit; sow a habit, reap a character; sow a character, reap a destiny" (Emerson). "Therefore let us think well. This is the principle of all morality" (Pascal).

Yet this is the area in which many demand freedom rather than obedience—as if God had a right to control my actions but not my thoughts, as if it were un-American for God to interfere with my "freedom of thought."

14. Another un-American virtue taught by St. Paul and all the saints, is detachment from worldly ambitions. While exactly contrary to what the world thinks, this is the secret of happiness and contentment: "... I have learned, in whatever state I am, to be content. I know how to be abased, and I know how to abound..." (4:11-12).

The two most important lessons in any game are how to be a good loser and how to be a good winner. And worldly ambition is only a game for Christians. That does not mean that we cannot play the game like any one else—with passion.

15. For all "losers," for all the weak, for "little" Christians, Paul offers the amazing claim of 4:13: "I can do all things in him who strengthens me." The answer to the question: how much can we do? is the answer to the question: how much can Christ do? For we are "in Christ," branches of that one vine. "All" is no exaggeration: "... with God all things are possible" (Mt 19:26).

16. But how much will he do for us? Like Jesus, Paul makes the astoundingly unqualified promise, "My God will supply every need of yours..." (4:19). This is reasonable, believe it or not. The reason is that the supply is "according to his riches in glory in Christ Jesus" (compare Rom 8:28-39).

Of course, he does not say that God will give us everything we *want*—unless what we want is identical with what we need. Christ-mindedness, the most pervasive theme of *Philippians,* means learning to bring our wants into alignment with our needs by learning to bring our minds into alignment with the mind of Christ. Insofar as we do this, it is inevitable that we will experience more of the power and the contentment that this saint writes of so eloquently and effortlessly.

Such effortless eloquence comes only from experience. Sanctity cannot be taught, like theology—only caught, like measles. The more we expose ourselves to highly contagious words like these, the more likely it is that we will be increasingly infected. They are words to get under our skin, under our conscious minds, into our memories and our hearts.

SIXTEEN

Christ, the Fullness of God: Colossians

COLOSSIANS IS SIMPLY COLOSSAL. It is about how big Christ is. How big is that? Pascal said, "Without Christ we cannot know the meaning of life, or death, or God, or ourselves." Those are the four most important questions there are.

Colossians is even more colossal than *Ephesians*. *Ephesians* is about the greatness of the body of Christ. *Colossians* is about the greatness of the Head.

Paul's basic answer in *Colossians* to this basic question: how big is Christ? is the key passage of 1:15-20. It says that Christ is no less than the full and complete expression of God, the source and purpose of the whole universe, the Savior and center of all things in Heaven and earth.

"He is the image of the invisible God, the firstborn of all creation; for in him all things were created, in heaven and on earth, visible and invisible, whether thrones or dominions, or principalities or authorities—all things were created through him and for him. He is before all things and in him all things hold together. He is the head of the body, the church; he is the beginning, the first-born from the dead, that in everything he may be preeminent. For in him all the fullness of God was pleased to dwell, and through him to reconcile to himself all things, whether on earth or in heaven, making peace by the blood of his cross."

Like most of Paul's letters, *Colossians* is divided into two parts: first doctrine (ch.s 1 and 2), then practice (ch.s 3 and 4). The two are connected, as is everything, by Christ: because Christ *is* the center of everything (the fundamental doctrine), Christians must *put* him first in everything (the fundamental practical point). Because he is the center of reality, he must be the center of our lives.

This connection can be seen in Paul's little transition words, which he puts at the beginning of the following key sentences in chapter 1. Because *"he is* the image of the invisible God" (v. 15), because *"he is* before all things" (v. 17), because *"he is* the head" (v. 18), therefore Paul concludes, *"And you,* who were once estranged... he has now reconciled... to present you holy" (vv. 21-22). The basic moral point of *Colossians* is that we must live according to this vision of ourselves in the colossal cosmic Christ.

The argument is this: (1) Christ is divine. (2) And you are in Christ. (3) Therefore, "if then you have been raised with Christ... set your minds on the things that are above, not on things that are on earth. For you have died, and your life is hid with Christ in God" (3:1-3).

What a liberation: we are already dead! Old Adam died with Christ on the cross and was buried with Christ in baptism. Now "... it is no longer I who live, *but Christ* who lives in me..." (Gal 2:20, emphasis mine).

The Church at Colossae was infected with an early form of gnosticism. Gnosticism, the popular Greek philosophical religion of the day, became the source of just about all the heresies in the early Church. In modern forms, it is still the source of most heresies today. At least five elements of the gnostic heresy can be seen in Colossians:

1. It confused Christianity with the speculations of Greek philosophy (2:4-10).
2. It confused Christianity with legalism, inherited from branches of Judaism which insisted on circumcision and strict dietary laws (2:11-17).

3. It confused Christianity with mysticism, visions, and experiences (2:18).
4. It confused Christianity with occult lore, which involved the idolatrous and superstitious worship of angels as mediators or intermediaries with God (2:20).
5. It confused Christianity with ascetic views and practices which sought to flee matter, the body, and the physical world (2:21-23).

Just as the Church would do for the next two thousand years, Paul said no to these little heresies because he knew how big Christ was. Whenever the Church condemns a heresy, it is for this reason. All heresies *reduce* Christ. The Church, however, knows how big Christ is and out of love and loyalty will not tolerate such narrow-mindedness and reductionism.

Gnosticism displaced Christ from the center and replaced him with five small things: speculation, legalism, mysticism, occultism, and asceticism. So Paul first states the truth positively about who Christ is (1:15-20). Then, in that light, he condemns the gnostic heretical theories (ch. 2). Finally, he applies this vision to daily life. After refuting gnosticism doctrinally, he refutes it practically, showing that Christian doctrine and practice, orthodoxy and orthopraxy, are inseparable.

All heresies are answered by one truth: Christ, "the way, the truth, and the life" (Jn 14:6). All heresies deny or reduce something about the complete Christ or the Christian's completeness in Christ.

These are the two fundamental themes of *Colossians* because they are the two fundamental themes of the whole Christian life:

1. "Christ, in whom are hid all the treasures of wisdom and knowledge" (2:3), "for in him the whole fulness of deity dwells bodily" (2:9);
2. "And you have come to fulness of life in him" (2:10).

In his *Soliloquies,* St. Augustine dialogues with his own reason and seeks to know only two things—the only two things we absolutely need to know because they are the only two things we can never, to all eternity, escape or avoid. *Colossians* supplies these two things:

> Augustine: Behold, I have prayed to God.
> Reason: What, then, do you desire to know?
> Augustine: Those things for which I have prayed.
> Reason: Sum them up, briefly.
> Augustine: I desire to know God and my soul.
> Reason: Nothing more?
> Augustine: Nothing more.

You can know God without knowing yourself. You can know yourself without knowing God. But you cannot know Christ without knowing both, and you cannot know either without knowing Christ.

SEVENTEEN

How to Misunderstand the Second Coming: First and Second Thessalonians

FIRST THESSALONIANS: LIVING IN NEWNESS OF LIFE AS WE AWAIT HIS COMING

Thessalonica was a major city in Macedonia (northern Greece). It was near Mount Olympus, fabled home of the Greek gods. The city still stands today. It is called Salonica.

Because the congregation contained both Greek and Hebrew members, Paul began his first letter to them with his usual greeting combining the Greek "grace" (*charis*) and the Hebrew "peace" (*shalom*). His letter is generally one of personal encouragement. It contains just one important doctrinal passage (4:13-5:11). But this passage is one of the most important and explicit passages in the Bible about Christ's Second Coming at the end of the world.

We would not have you ignorant, brethren, concerning those who are asleep, that you may not grieve as others do who have no hope.... For this we declare to you by the word of the Lord, that we who are alive, who are left until the coming of the Lord, shall not precede those who have fallen asleep. For the Lord himself will descend from heaven with a cry of command, with the archangel's call, and with the sound of the trumpet of God. And the dead in Christ will rise first; then we who are alive, who are left, shall be caught up together with them in the clouds to meet the Lord in the air; and so we shall always be with the Lord. Therefore comfort one another with these words.

These words are not merely comfort, they are also *true*. Paul is not telling fairy tales to children. The issue is serious. It is a matter of life and death. For it is the meaning of death and, therefore, the meaning and end of life. The Thessalonians had apparently become distressed over the death of some of their members. Paul comforts them with the truth that all believers in Christ will be united and resurrected at the Second Coming. Paul was very clear about the literalness and the absolute necessity of the resurrection: "If Christ has not been raised, then our preaching is in vain and your faith is in vain" (1 Cor 15:14).

In *1 Thessalonians*, as in all his letters, Paul joins doctrine and practice, dogma and ethics, theology and morality (the two things the Church is entrusted to teach infallibly). His connecting point here is that since we will live again in resurrected form when Christ comes, we should live now in newness of life in readiness and preparation for that event. Life is a rehearsal (*meleté*) for that great event. The play gives meaning to the rehearsal.

This means at least eight specific things and practical consequences in the present life as we prepare for the Second Coming:

1. hope, encouragement, and comfort (4:18);
2. alertness, open-eyed expectation (5:4);
3. firmness, "stand[ing] fast in the Lord" (3:8);
4. critical questioning (5:21: "Test everything, hold fast what is good");
5. sobriety, both mental and physical (5:6) (Imagine Christ coming and finding you too drunk to recognize him!);

and the three universal responses of 5:16-18:

6. "rejoice always";
7. "pray constantly";
8. "give thanks in all things, for this is the will of God in Christ Jesus for you" (see Rom 8:28).

Everything in our lives should be transformed by this hope of our ultimate end. The best practical way to discern whether anything is good or evil is to ask: would I want Jesus to find me doing this when he comes again? The Second Coming is not a strange myth to be tucked away in some remote corner of our mind, but a truth to be lived daily, like everything in the Bible. God's revelation is not misty-eyed escapism but clear-eyed realism. For no event in history is as important, as spectacular, or as final as that ultimate event, "when the Lord Jesus is revealed from heaven with his mighty angels in flaming fire" (2 Thess 1:7).

SECOND THESSALONIANS: THE DISASTROUS EFFECTS OF MISUNDERSTANDING THE SECOND COMING

Paul's *Second Letter to the Thessalonians* is the second stage of the story of his trying to teach the Thessalonians the real implications of the doctrine of the Second Coming. It is essential to get this doctrine right, for it is close to center stage in the Christian Gospel. It is mentioned no less than three hundred and eighteen times in the New Testament!

The Thessalonians had misunderstood Paul's teaching in two ways.

First, they seem to have thought they knew how soon Christ would come, even though Christ himself did not (Matt 24:36) and even though Paul too had told them that the Lord would come not when expected but "like a thief in the night" (1 Thes 5:2).

Second, some had given up their jobs and were just waiting around until the end, even though Paul had explicitly warned them about this in *1 Thessalonians* 4:11-12: "… aspire to live quietly, to mind your own affairs, and to work with your hands, as we charged you, so that you may command the respect of outsiders and be dependent on nobody." But Paul had to repeat his warning against idleness in his second letter (3:6) and lay down the common sense economic principle (which is no longer common sense today), "If anyone will not work, let him not eat" (3:10). (This was not universally recognized in Paul's day either; Rome was soon to grow into a swollen welfare state of "bread and circuses.")

It is enlightening to see the oneness of orthodoxy and orthopraxy, right doctrine and right life, throughout the New Testament. The Thessalonians' misunderstanding of the doctrine of the Second Coming necessarily had disastrous effects in their lives.

Even today this doctrine is more of a touchstone of orthodoxy than most of us realize. The mistake Paul corrects in *1 Thessalonians* is essentially the same mistake that is made by modernism: ignoring, denying, or reducing to myth and symbolism the Second Coming. And the mistake Paul corrects in *2 Thessalonians*, apparently made in misunderstanding Paul's first letter, is essentially the same mistake that is made by many modern fundamentalists and extremist sects: a fixation and obsession with the imminence of the Second Coming.

Modernism tends to ignore the next life for this one. Fundamentalism tends to ignore this life for the next. But orthodoxy sees the two as mutually reinforcing, like life before birth and life after birth.

Paul uses the Old Testament term "the day of the Lord" to refer to Christ's Second Coming. In the Old Testament, this is a phrase full of mystery. What is clear about it is that it will be the time when God does his greatest work in history and inaugurates a radically new era. That no one understood very well just what that work was to be is shown by the fact that *no* one understood Christ when he came, neither his enemies nor his friends, not even his apostles. Even his mother was puzzled.

The term "day" (*yom* in Hebrew) does not necessarily mean a literal twenty-four hour day but a period of time, perhaps a very long time. The six "days" of creation in *Genesis* 1, for instance, took millions of years. When Paul spoke of "the day of the Lord" to the Thessalonians he meant the last times, the last era in world history. In one sense this era had come already with Christ's first coming. Yet in another sense (the one Paul emphasizes here), it had not yet come, for there are certain events that have to happen before the end, such as the appearance of "the man of lawlessness... the son of perdition," that is, the Antichrist (2:3).

The correct practical results of correct belief about Christ's coming "like a thief in the night" should be to work for our salvation, for others' welfare, and above all for their salvation through the spread of the good news throughout the world while there is still time. This is just the opposite of laziness and passivity. It means not leaving your job but taking on a new job. If every Christian lived out his essential missionary vocation, the world would be reconverted in two generations.

Since we do not know the day or the hour, we must be ready at any time, not by doing nothing but by doing everything we are called to do, by knowing and doing the whole of God's will for us. As a bumper sticker on a college campus put it, "Prepare for your finals: read your Bible."

EIGHTEEN

Letters to Paul's Helpers: First Timothy, Second Timothy, and Titus

FIRST TIMOTHY: "HOW TO BE A BISHOP"

Timothy was a young convert via Paul's preaching. He became the bishop of the important city of Ephesus while still young. Paul wrote this letter to him personally for encouragement and advice on how to administer this great responsibility. The title could be "How to Be a Bishop."

There were problems in the Church at Ephesus (where aren't there?). Some members needed discipline, widows and old people were being neglected, and there was false teaching. Timothy was apparently having a difficult time dealing with these problems because he was young (4:12), sickly (5:23), and timid (2 Tm 1:7). Paul encourages him to "fight the good fight of the faith" (6:12).

The qualifications for a bishop mentioned in this letter are not worldly administrative or organizational skills, but personal piety and spiritual strength (3:1-13). The same is true even for the more practical office of deacon.

Ten notable passages are the following:

1. *First Timothy* 2:9-15 is perhaps the most hated passage in Scripture to feminists. Women are forbidden to have

authority over men in the church. They are commanded to be silent, submissive, and modest in dress. That seems pretty clear, however unpopular. Less clear is the assertion that "woman will be saved through bearing children" (2:15). The one thing that should be clear is that this exalts the uniquely feminine work rather than demeaning it. Those who interpret Paul in the latter way reveal nothing about him but much about themselves.

2. The passage of 3:4-5 makes clear that it was normal for bishops at this time to be married.

3. *First Timothy* 3:16 seems to be an early creed: "... the mystery of our religion: He was manifested in the flesh, vindicated in the Spirit, seen by angels, preached among the nations, believed on in the world, taken up in glory."

4. The passage of 4:1 speaks of the middle of the first century as already "the last days," and already full of heresies, especially gnosticism (4:3-4), with its attack on nature, especially marriage. Radical feminism corresponds exactly to ancient gnosticism in every way (except gnosticism's disapproval of sexual promiscuity).

5. *First Timothy* 4:8 should prove an embarrassing verse to modern health fanatics.

6. The passage of 4:14 speaks of the Sacrament of Holy Orders.

7. *First Timothy* 5:8 is a stronger version of "charity begins at home": "If anyone does not provide for his relatives and especially for his own family, he has disowned the faith and is worse than an unbeliever."

8. The passage of 5:23 threatens the principle of teetotalling for everyone. Note, however, that Paul recommends *only a little* wine.

9. *First Timothy* 6:6-8 is the famous, well-loved "contentment" passage: "There is great gain in godliness with contentment; for we brought nothing into the world and we cannot take anything out of the world; but if we

have food and clothing, with these we shall be content.... For the love of money is the root of all evils."
Jesus said the same thing many times and surprised his
disciples then as he surprises us now.

10. The passage of 6:16 reveals two things about God that
may be surprising. First, he alone is immortal by nature.
(We are immortal not by nature, as Plato thought, but
by grace, through the miracle of resurrection.) Second,
he "dwells in unapproachable light, whom no man has
ever seen or can see." God is *I AM*, pure Subject, not the
object of our knowing. He is "the I who can never become an It" (Buber). We know him only because he has
revealed himself (see Jn 1:18).

SECOND TIMOTHY: A LETTER OF ENCOURAGEMENT

Paul wrote this second letter to Timothy from prison,
awaiting execution. Christianity had become illegal in the
Roman Empire since the sadistic and insane Nero had
blamed the Christians for the great fire which burned half of
Rome in A.D. 64—a fire he probably caused himself. The persecutions and martyrdoms had begun. Paul's enemies used
this opportunity to get him arrested.

When he wrote this letter, Paul had no hope of being res-
cued (4:6-8, 18). He asked Timothy to visit him before he was
killed (4:9-21). He complains that everyone had abandoned
him, except for Luke (4:10-11).

The first time Paul had been arrested, it had been only a
house arrest. He had hope of release or trial, and he was free
to preach to friends who visited him (Acts 28:16-31). Now he
had only death to look forward to—or rather, something
much better than death, and better than this life (4:6-8).

From his prison Paul writes not complaints but encourage-
ments to Timothy, and warns him that he will have to endure
hardships and persecutions too, not only from Roman

authorities but also from false teachers within the Church. He encourages Timothy to overcome his timidity and youth (1:5-9). Paul's language is very strong (as I think it would be today if he were writing to certain contemporary bishops who are over-timid and try to be popular): "I charge you in the presence of God and of Christ Jesus who is to judge the living and the dead... preach the word, be urgent in season and out of season" [when convenient and inconvenient, when popular and unpopular] (4:1-2). "Share in suffering as a good soldier of Christ Jesus" (2:3). The idea of spiritual warfare and of being persecuted for the faith is on just about every page Paul ever wrote.

Christianity has always flourished under persecution. "The blood of the martyrs is the seed of the Church." The cross is the strongest force in the world. Spilled blood has more power than split atoms. The strongest churches today are still found in countries where it costs something to be a Christian.

Timothy's weapon that guarantees him success is truth, found in God's Word (see Jn 17:17). *Second Timothy* 3:14-17 is Scripture's classic passage about itself. Other memorable passages include the following:

1. *Second Timothy* 1:12 is a great expression of Christian confidence and boldness: "I am not ashamed, for I know whom I have believed, and I am sure that he is able to guard until that Day what has been entrusted to me."

2. The passage of 2:15 is the Christian teacher's job description: "Do your best to present yourself to God as one approved, a workman who has no need to be ashamed, rightly handling the word of truth."

3. *Second Timothy* 3:1-7 sounds like a prophecy of twentieth century moral and intellectual decadence.

4. The passage of 3:12 is a universal promise of persecution: "all who desire to live a godly life in Christ Jesus will be persecuted." Therefore, if we are not being persecuted, we can deduce what logically follows from that fact.

5. *Second Timothy* 4:7-8 is Paul's own self-composed epitaph: "I have fought the good fight, I have finished the race, I have kept the faith. Henceforth there is laid up for me the crown of righteousness, which the Lord, the righteous judge, will award to me on that Day, and not only to me but also to all who have loved his appearing." May every reader be able honestly to engrave that on his or her gravestone.

TITUS: A LETTER OF ADVICE

Like Timothy, Titus was a young pastor with a difficult responsibility: the Church in Crete. The inhabitants of this Mediterranean island were famous for immorality; in fact, Paul quotes Epimenides the Cretan poet who had written six centuries earlier, "Cretans are always liars, evil beasts, and lazy gluttons" (1:12). "To act like a Cretan" was a saying in the ancient world that means "to be a liar."

Titus has to organize the Christian Church in Crete. Paul writes some good advice to him. First, as a bishop himself, Titus should appoint other bishops who are of strong moral character, who *practice* what they preach. Then Paul advises Titus to exercise his authority firmly (perhaps Titus, like Timothy, tended to be timid), refuting false teachers and forbidding evil deeds. For the Church, as we have seen, needs both orthodoxy (right belief) and orthopraxis (right practice), and the two are always connected.

The strong note of *authority* in Paul, here as in his other letters, should not be misunderstood. It is not sheer power or bullying, but speaking in the name of Christ, who himself spoke "with authority" (Mt 7:29) and who commissioned his followers to preach in his name and his authority (Mt 28:18-20). It is not *might* but *right,* "with firmness in the right." Paul's attitude to false teaching and practice is neither "burn the heretics" nor "anything goes," but "what does Jesus say?"

NINETEEN

A Personal and Tender Letter to a Friend: Philemon

THIS SHORTEST OF ALL Paul's letters (it could fit on a postcard) is to many readers the most personal, simple, direct, and appealing of all. There is a dramatic and poignant story behind it.

Onesimus, a slave, had run away from his master, Philemon, who was a friend and convert of Paul's. Onesimus had made his way to Rome and to Paul. There he had come to faith in Christ through Paul's influence (v. 10). Now Paul sends him back to his master with this note, telling Philemon to forgive him and accept him back not as a slave but as a brother in Christ (v. 16).

By Roman law, a runaway slave could be killed. Only because he was now a Christian would Onesimus think of voluntarily returning to his master. Only because Philemon was a Christian would he forgive and free Onesimus, as Paul suggests (vv. 16-17).

The letter is full of tact and tenderness, and also wit. Verse 11 is a pun on the name "Onesimus," which means "useful." Onesimus had proved useless to Philemon by deserting him, but now he is "useful" to both Paul and Philemon. Paul asks Philemon to treat Onesimus as he would treat Paul himself (v. 17). He promises to repay any debt Onesimus may owe. The parallel to Christ is obvious, and Paul is confident that this Christ-like example will win Philemon's good will.

There is deep religious significance in this little personal drama. It shows how relationships are transformed by Christ from slavery to freedom, from bondage to brotherhood. It shows how Christians who have been freed and forgiven by Christ must free and forgive others, how Christians should set aside their rights (vv. 8-9) to serve others as Christ set aside his rights to serve us, and how Christians should pay each other's debts as Christ paid our debt of sin.

Love goes far beyond justice, grace far beyond law. Like us, Onesimus is saved only by grace. Like Christ, Paul pays and forgives his debt. Like God the Father, Philemon accepts this substitution and takes back his runaway as a member of his family. It is a perfect object lesson of theology-in-life, Christianity-in-practice.

TWENTY

Christ as Prophet, Priest, and King: Hebrews

N O ONE BUT GOD KNOWS who wrote *Hebrews*, or to whom. The clue in 13:23 seems to point to St. Paul. But for a variety of reasons, most scholars no longer hold to Pauline authorship of *Hebrews*. However, the jury is still out.

Hebrews seems to be addressed to Jewish Christians who were undergoing persecution for their new belief and were tempted to abandon their faith in Christ under this severe testing (10:32-34), though it had not yet reached the point of martyrdom (12:4). The author argues the need to hold fast to Christ as Lord and Savior—the very essence of Christianity.

As *Romans* is the world's first *systematic theology*, *Hebrews* is the first *apologetic* for the Christian faith. "Apologetic" here does not mean "excuse" but "defense"; not "I was wrong" but "I am right." *Hebrews* argues for the superiority of Christ in every way to Judaism, to prevent Jewish Christians from choosing the shadow over the substance, the promises over their fulfillment, the arrow over the bull's-eye.

The author emphasizes Christ's threefold office as prophet, priest, and king—the three Old Testament offices that fore-shadowed him. It emphasizes both his divinity (1:1-8) and his humanity (2:9-10; 2:14-18; 4:15; 5:7-9; 12:3; 13:12). The overall theme is like that of *Colossians:* the all-sufficient greatness of Christ (compare *Hebrews* 1:3 with *Colossians* 1:15-20).

Along with *Genesis, 1 John,* and *John's Gospel, Hebrews* begins with one of the four great first verses in the Bible, which reveal a total sweep of history: "In many and various ways God spoke of old to our fathers by the prophets; but in these last days he has spoken to us by a Son...." This beginning sets the theme for the whole book: Judaism is not so much *wrong* as *fulfilled and completed,* in Christ and the Church through whom God has spoken a new Word. The author constantly quotes God's (Old Testament) Word, as Matthew does, for a similar purpose (to convince and convert Jews). He has a high, holy, and practical attitude of existential urgency toward the Word. It is not just "proof texts" but the present, living speech of the present, living God. "Take care, brethren.... 'Today, when you hear his voice, do not harden your hearts....'" (3:12,15). This Word is described (in 4:12-13) as "living and active, sharper than any two-edged sword, piercing to the division of soul and spirit [do you know that difference?], of joints and marrow, and discerning the thoughts and intentions of the heart. And before him no creature is hidden, but all are open and laid bare to the eyes of him with whom we have to do."

The whole point of the Old Testament Word, according to *Hebrews,* is to point to Christ. It is incomplete in itself (11:39-40). The old and new covenants are strikingly contrasted in 12:18-24, as Paul contrasts law and grace in *Romans.* By the way, the more I compare *Hebrews* and Paul's letters, the more I see Paul in *Hebrews*—if not his authorship, at least his doctrine.

Christ is shown to be superior in every way:

1. He is superior to angels, for they worship him (1:4-2:18).
2. He is superior to Moses and Joshua, for they are creatures, while he is the Creator (3:1-4:13).
3. He is a better priest than the human priest Aaron, for his sacrifice was once for all (8:1-10:18). His priesthood

is greater than that of Levi, akin to the priesthood of Melchizedek (4:14-7:28). The Old Testament priest-hood and liturgy were *symbolic* of Christ and of Heaven (8:1-5).

It needs to be pointed out here that the medieval penchant for interpreting Scripture symbolically is rooted in Scripture itself. Some modern exegetes turn it upside down and interpret symbolically not the symbol (the Old Testament) but the reality symbolized (Christ's divinity, resurrection, atonement, and Second Coming).

4. He is superior to the old law, or old covenant, for his blood takes away our sin (8:1-10:39). As a consequence, we have real, objective access to God, and felt, subjective confidence (10:19-20).

The most famous chapter in *Hebrews* is chapter 11, the great roll call of the heroes of faith, the Christian hall of fame. It begins with the famous description of faith itself (v. 1): "Now faith is the assurance of things hoped for, the conviction of things not seen." See the passage 2:8-9: "As it is, we do not yet see everything in subjection to him. But we see Jesus...." Faith goes beyond the seen, but it begins there. It is not like a blind date but like a marriage.

The faith-works controversy is solved (without even being posed) by seeing faith as a thing that *works*, that acts. "*By faith* Abraham obeyed... *By faith* the people crossed the Red Sea. ... *By faith* the walls of Jericho fell down... *through faith* [they] conquered kingdoms, enforced justice, received promises, stopped the mouths of lions..." (11:8, 29, 30, 33, emphasis mine).

Faith and hope are virtually identified in the passages 11:1 and 11:14-16. Here faith includes hope. In *1 Peter* 3:15, hope includes faith. Hope *is* faith directed to the future.

Chapter 12 is the practical conclusion and exhortation from chapter 11: "Therefore, since we are surrounded by so great a cloud of witnesses, let us also lay aside every weight

and sin which clings so closely, and let us run with persever-
ance the race that is set before us, looking to Jesus the pio-
neer and perfecter of our faith, who for the joy that was set
before him endured the cross, despising the shame, and is
seated at the right hand of the throne of God" (12:1-2). The
Greek word for "witnesses" means (1) martyrs, (2) those who
testify, as in court, and (3) those who see or observe, imply-
ing that these saints are now watching us from Heaven. How
would you feel if you saw thousands of eyes outside your
window?

There is a weighty consequence to such a weighty theology
of such a weighty Christ: "How shall we escape if we neglect
such a great salvation?" (2:3). No more urgent and heart-
stoppingly serious passage exists in all the world's literature
than *Hebrews* 12:25-29. It concludes with a vision of God's
essential nature as "fire," just as Moses saw him in the burning
bush, and as Pascal saw him on the night he met him: "God of
Abraham, Isaac, and Jacob, not the God of philosophers and
scholars" (*Pensées* 913). As Rabbi Abraham Heschel says, "God
is not nice. God in not an uncle. God is an earthquake." Or as
C.S. Lewis says of his Christ-figure Aslan, "He's not tame. But
he's *good.*" Goodness is not tame. The essential root of modernist theology is right there, in the *taming* of God.

Chapter 12 also contains one of the greatest exhortations
on suffering and its meaning ever written (vv. 5-12). This
short passage says more about life's most popular problem
than most complete books on the subject.

Chapter 13 gives us one of Scripture's many classic passages on the need to be countercultural (vv. 11-14). This is as
necessary today as nineteen centuries ago, for the only difference between the old, pre-Christian paganism and the new,
post-Christian paganism is that the new is worse because it
knows more and is more responsible.

Other not-to-be-missed gems in this diamond mine of a
book include the following passages, all of them surprising

points to learn something new from, not soporific reinforcements of what we all know already:

- *Hebrews* 2:11, on our participation in divine life (compare Jn 15:5; 2 Pt 1:4);
- The passage of 2:14-15, on how Christ destroys not only death but also the *fear* of death and the bondage this fear keeps us in (what we really fear is not death but Hell!);
- *Hebrews* 2:18, on how fully and thoroughly human Christ is;
- The passage of 5:8, on how even Christ had to learn obedience through suffering (George MacDonald says, "Christ suffered, not that we may be freed from suffering but that our suffering may be changed into his");
- *Hebrews* 6:5, on how we already taste "the powers of the age to come" (Heaven), like appetizers;
- The passage of 9:22, on the need for death and blood and sacrifice to take away sin—contrary to modern, "enlightened" religion, every ancient religion knew this in its bones;
- *Hebrews* 9:27, a definitive disproof of reincarnation;
- The passage of 13:2, on the sacred nature of hospitality and the disturbing proximity of angels;
- *Hebrews* 13:8, on God's opinion of "new" Christianities.

The central theme and thread holding all these pearls together is the center of all reality, Christ. *Hebrews*' essential message is life's essential message: "Let us keep our eyes fixed on Jesus" (12:2 NEV), for "Jesus Christ is the same yesterday and today and forever" (13:8). In the words of the great old hymn, "The Church's one foundation is Jesus Christ her Lord." *Hebrews* goes down to bedrock.

TWENTY-ONE

Doers of the Word: James

T HE AUTHOR OF the *Epistle of James* was probably not the James who was one of Jesus' twelve apostles, John's brother. That James was martyred very early, probably in A.D. 44 (Acts 12:2). The author was probably the James who was one of Jesus' "brothers" mentioned in *Matthew* 13:55. (The Hebrew word translated "brothers" can also mean "cousins" or "relatives.")

Since God's people were scattered—or dispersed—over the whole world, James, Peter, John, and Jude all wrote "general epistles," that is, letters "to the twelve tribes in the Dispersion" (1:1) rather than to any one local church, as Paul did in his letters.

James' letter is like the *Book of Proverbs* in the Old Testament: full of maxims and practical advice about living. It is not primarily doctrinal and does not have a systematic outline. But its unifying theme is 1:22: "Be doers of the word, and not hearers only...." Orthodoxy must be supplemented by orthopraxy.

The most famous and important passage in *James* is 2: 14-26, about faith and works. Martin Luther denied that *James* belonged in the Bible because he could not reconcile James' emphasis on works with Paul's emphasis on faith.

But faith and works are not opposites. That is James' whole point! They are complementary, like the root and the flower of a single plant. James' point is that a faith that does not produce good works is not true faith, but dead faith (2:17), like a plant that produces no flowers or seeds.

Actually, James' point is very clear and simple. It is not a contrast between faith and works but between a real faith, a faith that works, and a false faith, one that does not. "Show me your faith apart from your works, and I by my works will show you my faith." We do not see a living plant's roots, only its fruits. Others cannot see your faith, for it is invisible. They can only see your actions, which show your faith as a tulip flower shows you that a tulip bulb has taken root.

The apparent contradiction between James, who says that we, like Abraham, are justified by works (2:21), and Paul, who says that we, like Abraham, are justified by faith (Rom 4), is explained by seeing these two things as two sides of the same coin.

It is further explained by looking at the context. Paul's context is the relationship between the believer and God, while James' context is the relationship between the believer and his neighbor. God sees your faith; your neighbor sees and is touched by your works. Faith justifies us before God; works justify us before our neighbors.

A further explanation is that James means by "faith" only intellectual belief. "You believe that God is one; you do well. Even the demons believe—and shudder" (2:19). But Paul means by "faith" (in *Galatians* and *Romans*) the whole Christian life.

In more technical terms, Paul is contrasting faith with law as a way to be justified, while James is contrasting a faith without works with a faith that works as a way to be sanctified. Paul is asking how to be saved; James is asking how to be holy. Paul is asking how to get to Heaven, James is asking how to live on earth.

In any case, the "bottom line" is that faith and works are

two aspects of the very same reality: the new birth, the super-natural life of God, which enters the soul by faith and comes out as the works of love. "You see that faith was active along with his works, and faith was completed by works..." (2:22).

James also mentions ten other things that faith does: (1) it endures sufferings and trials, (2) it obeys the word of God that it hears, (3) it overcomes favoritism and prejudice, (4) it controls the tongue and gossip, (5) it gives us wisdom, (6) it separates us from the world, (7) it makes us submissive to God, (8) it resists the devil, (9) it puts us in God's presence, and (10) it waits patiently for Christ's Second Coming. *James* never teaches works *versus* faith or works *instead* of faith. From beginning to end, the letter is a tribute to faith, but to a faith that works, like the one described in *Hebrews* 11.

Some unique features of *James* include the promise of the supernatural gift of wisdom (1:5), the holistic interpretation of the law (2:10-11), a scary verse for teachers (3:1), an answer to what is the most dangerous and uncontrollable organ in your body (3:3-12), the solution to the puzzle of the origin of war (4:1-3), and the scriptural basis of the Sacrament of the Sick (5:13-18).

Memorable reiterations of doctrines taught many other times in Scripture include the passages of 1:2 (on suffering), 1:17 (on grace), 4:4 (on worldliness), 4:7-8 (on dealing with the devil), 4:8 and 5:8-9 (on purity of heart: see Kierkegaard's great title, *Purity of Heart Is to Will One Thing*), 5:13-15 (on playing God versus trusting Providence), and 5:12 (on straightforward, simple honesty—if only the "nuancers" would read that and *Matthew* 5:37).

Each of his apostles emphasized a different aspect of Christ. James, like Mark, emphasized his practicality. This is the epistle theoreticians and scholars like the least and need the most.

TWENTY-TWO

Standing Fast in Christ: Letters of Peter

P ETER'S TWO LETTERS COULD BE CALLED "Rocky I" and "Rocky II," for Jesus had declared Peter to be the Rock on which he would build his Church (Mt 16:18). We see in them not the "sandy" Peter of the Gospels, the Peter with foot-in-mouth disease, but a rock-solid saint. His two letters are full of sound advice and exhortations for daily Christian living. Peter's letters, like James', are practical. Paul's letters, like John's, are more intellectual. Peter and James are exhortatory; Paul and John are expository.

There is no "Rocky III" because Peter was martyred in Rome in or around A.D. 66. The prophecy Jesus had made about how Peter was to die (Jn 21:18-19) was fulfilled when Nero crucified Peter. Tradition says Peter insisted on being crucified upside down because he did not want to seem equal to his Master.

Peter wrote these two "general epistles" to Christians scattered throughout the empire, that is, the civilized world (1:1). Peter had taken the center of Church authority to the center of the world, Rome. He spent the last decade of his life there. He refers to Rome symbolically as "Babylon" (5:13), for Babylon was the traditional enemy of the Jews, the empire that had conquered and enslaved them six hundred years earlier just as Rome had done again. Now Rome was turning her hatred also on the new Israel, the Church, when Nero and Diocletian began persecuting Christians.

FIRST PETER: STAND FAST IN PERSECUTION

Peter writes his first letter to advise Christians how to deal with suffering abuse and persecution. The "fiery ordeal" (4:12) endured by these Christians outside Rome to whom Peter wrote was not yet martyrdom, for Nero's killings were confined to the city of Rome. Only later did they begin killing Christians throughout the empire. It was probably the scorns and sneers of their neighbors, who resented Christians for being different. It was becoming increasingly clear to the pagans, just as it is to the neo-pagans in our contemporary de-Christianized society, that Christians are a dangerously different people with a dangerously different Lord, love, and lifestyle.

This kind of persecution has not ended with the end of the Roman Empire, of course. As anyone knows who has seriously attempted it, *living* the whole Gospel in a fallen world can be harder than *dying* for it.

Yet Peter does not blame the state as an institution for its mistreatment of Christians. In fact, like Paul in *Romans* 13, he tells his readers to submit to its authority as divinely instituted and for God's sake (2:13-14). The state, like the whole world, is seen not as an opaque *thing* but as a door or window to and from God.

Peter's tone is full of grace and gentleness, and also hope and encouragement. He practices what he preaches about being a pastor (shepherd) of souls, an example rather than a lord (5:1-3; compare with Jn 13:12-17). Peter had finally learned Jesus' simple but shocking lesson and learned it well. Like Paul, he preaches service and submission: of citizens to the state, of servants to their masters, wives to their husbands, and generally of all Christians to each other (3:8).

Christian "submission" makes sense only if the state, master, husband, parent, or friend is seen as an icon of Christ. If we really believed our Lord's solemnly non-exaggerated words, "Truly, I say to you, as you did it to one of the least of these my brethren, you did it to me" (Mt 25:40), we would not balk at the idea of "submission."

There is a consistent teaching throughout the Bible, especially in the New Testament and the epistles, that the divine order for human society and relationships involves hierarchy, authority, and obedience. But the rivers that run in these hierarchical riverbeds are rivers of love and humility, not power (5:5; compare with Eph 5:21).

First Peter focuses most especially on the problem of suffering. Peter tells his flock three essential practical truths about Christian suffering:

First, that we should not be surprised at it: "Beloved, do not be surprised at the fiery ordeal which comes upon you to prove you, as though something strange were happening to you" (4:12). If the head suffers, his body must also suffer, for otherwise it is not his body. Christ never promised us a rose garden without thorns. Instead, he promised that "if they persecuted me, they will persecute you; if they kept my word, they will keep yours also" (Jn 15:20). George MacDonald says, "The Son of God suffered not so that we might not suffer but so that our sufferings might become his."

Second, because of this real incorporation into his body, suffering can be or become joy: "But rejoice in so far as you share Christ's sufferings, that you may also rejoice and be glad when his glory is revealed" (4:13). We must not be bitter or resentful to God for allowing us to suffer, but realize that sufferings are God's blessings, not his punishments. As St. Philip Neri said, "The cross is the gift God gives to his friends."

Third, there is an eschatological dimension to understanding suffering. "After you have suffered a little while, the God of all grace, who has called you to his eternal glory in Christ, will himself restore, establish, and strengthen you" (5:10). Suffering does not weaken us but strengthens us in the long run. The biblical answer to the problem of suffering is not some abstract, timeless truth but two real historical events: the two comings of Christ, one past, one future. The full answer is something that will happen when Christ returns. In this light, read and pray the passage of 1:3-10, probably the key passage to the whole letter.

Fourth, in order to transform suffering into joy by its incorporation into Christ, our sufferings must be for good, not for evil. Paradoxically, only unjust suffering is good; suffering justly is evil. "What credit is it if when you do wrong and are beaten for it you take it patiently? But if when you do right and suffer for it you take it patiently, you have God's approval" (2:20; compare with 4:1-16).

Other notable and memorable passages in this little letter include:

1. The charter of Christian apologetics: "Always be prepared to make a defense (*logos*, reason) to anyone who calls you to account for the hope that is in you" (3:15);
2. The promise that "love covers a multitude of sins" (4:8)—this is *agape*, not *eros*, of course—charity, not romance;
3. The unqualified exhortation to "cast *all* your anxieties on him, for he cares for you" (5:7);
4. The exhortation to "be sober, be watchful. Your adversary the devil prowls around like a roaring lion, seeking someone to devour. Resist him, firm in your faith" (5:8-9). This verse used to be very familiar, in the old days when the idea of spiritual warfare was as commonly taught in the Church as it is in the Scriptures. This passage was repeated every day in the daily Divine Office, prayed by all monks, most priests, and many of the laity.
5. The intriguing passage about Christ preaching to the dead "spirits in prison" (presumably Purgatory) who

had lived in Noah's time. This seems to be what Christ did between Good Friday and Easter Sunday. He was busy even then (see Jn 5:16-17)!

6. The simple statement that "baptism... saves you" (3:21). This is a very embarrassing one for many Protestants who teach that the sacraments are mere symbols.

SECOND PETER: STAND FAST AGAINST HERESY AND SIN

This letter was written just before Peter's anticipated death by martyrdom (1:14-15), between A.D. 62 and 66, from Rome. It is the last recorded words of the first recorded pope.

Peter refers to Paul's letters (3:15-16) as already well-known in the Church, thus proving they were written quite early. By the way, if you find Paul's writings difficult, you are in good company: so did Peter (3:16).

This short letter is Peter's "reminder" (1:12) of the familiar, essential Gospel truth and of its solid foundation in two public facts. Only Judaism and Christianity are religions of public record, eyewitnessed facts. All others are (pagan) myths, (Oriental) mysticisms, or (modernist) moralisms.

The two facts are (1) the disciples' and Peter's own eyewitness experience of Jesus (1:16-18) and (2) the written prophecies of Scripture which Jesus fulfilled: "For we did not follow cleverly devised myths when we made known to you the power and coming of our Lord Jesus Christ, but we were eyewitnesses of his majesty... And we have the prophetic word made more sure. You will do well to pay attention to this as to a lamp shining in a dark place, until the day dawns and the morning star arises in your hearts. First of all, you must understand that no prophecy of scripture is a matter of one's own interpretation, because no prophecy ever came by the impulse of man, but men moved by the Holy Spirit spoke from God" (1:16, 19-21). This passage seems clearly to reject both the modernist view of Scripture as *human* interpretation rather than divine intervention, and the Protestant principle of *private* interpretation.

Peter's first letter dealt with external dangers to the Church: persecution and sufferings. His second letter deals with internal dangers: heresies and sins. The early Church and the early Christians were being confused and harmed by false teaching. This is why the New Testament is so consistently harsh on false doctrine: down the road it always harms people, and Christians love people. It's out of liberal-hearted love and compassion for people that the Church has always been so hardheadedly conservative about doctrine.

Just as there were false as well as true prophets throughout the history of Israel, they persisted in the early Church. And not only the *early* Church. Does anyone really doubt who they are today? Who can read without embarrassment the many passages in Scripture denouncing false teachers, and who can't? Who do and who do not believe there *are* such things as false teachings because there are such things as objective truth and divine revelation?

Peter points out the connection between false doctrine and false practice. Orthodoxy (right belief) and orthopraxy (right practice) always stand or fall together. The saints are always orthodox. They are the consistent living refutation of all who say orthopraxy alone is enough— *or* orthodoxy alone.

For just as true doctrine naturally produces true living (since good works are the fruit of faith; see *James*), false doctrine always produces false living: licentiousness (2:2), greed (2:3), arrogance and the despising of authority (2:10), lust (2:10, 13, 14), and a false "freedom." "They promise them freedom, but they themselves are slaves of corruption; for whatever overcomes a man, to that he is enslaved" (2:19). As George MacDonald put it, "A man is a slave to whatever he cannot part with that is less than himself."

These false teachers were also scoffing at the belief that Christ would return to judge them (3:3-10). Peter writes some very disturbingly strong words against these teachers, just as Jesus used similar words against the Pharisees and scribes—not out of hatred but out of the kind of "tough love" that shouts "Danger!" when someone is near the edge of a cliff or on thin ice.

For God cannot change his essential nature, which is both love and justice. He delays his punishments to give us time to repent (3:9-15), but punishment for sin is inevitable (2:4-6; 3:9, 12, 17). This is a theme taught on every page of Scripture, yet one hardly taught on a single page of modern books of "religious education." The God of infinite and unchangeable love cast his rebel angels into Hell, destroyed the world with a flood, and rained fire and brimstone on Sodom and Gomorrah. It is not possible that he will wink sleepily at New York or Belfast.

The best antidote for Christians against heresies is the positive one: understanding the truth. That is why Peter the Rock writes this reminder of the foundations of the faith (1:12-13; 3:1-2). "Reminding" is the business of the magisterium and the papacy, the Rock. Buildings with a strong rock as their foundation, like those on Manhattan Island, can grow to skyscrapers. A foundation *has* to be conservative, a "stick-in-the-mud," like an anchor.

Also included in *2 Peter* is the most explicit passage in Scripture about the most high, exalted, and incredible destiny of believers to actually share God's nature: "... he has granted to us his precious and very great promises, that through these you may escape from the corruption that is in the world because of passion, and become partakers of the divine nature" (1:3-4). It is only in light of this our revealed destiny and ultimate identity that the uncompromisingly idealistic, otherworldly, and countercultural moral exhortations found in every book of the New Testament make perfect sense.

A Spiritual Father Writes to His Children: Letters of John

FIRST JOHN: SHARING GOD'S VERY LIFE

This beautiful letter was written by the apostle John in his old age to his spiritual "children," Christians who were not beginners but already mature in their faith (2:7; 2:18-27; 3:11). Like his Gospel, this letter is profound. Yet it is simple. It is deep, yet clear enough for a child to understand it.

One of John's purposes is to combat gnosticism. Gnosticism taught that matter was evil, that God had not created the material world, and that Jesus could not possibly be God incarnate. Gnostics believed that their new, super-spiritualized version of Christianity was the superior "hidden knowledge" (*gnosis*). They thought that only the uneducated masses would believe the literal incarnational and traditional faith as expressed in the Gospels and by the Church. They also thought they had a superior morality, which elevated them above the ordinary distinctions between right and wrong, good and evil.

Positively, the fundamental theme of John's letter is the essence of religion: a relationship with God, union with God, fellowship with God, sharing God's life. John wants us to be certain and assured of our relationship with God, of our eternal life: "I write this to you who believe in the name of the Son of God, that you may know that you have eternal life" (5:13). The basis of our certainty is not ourselves but Jesus: "He who has the Son has life; he who has not the Son of God has not life" (5:12). It is as simple as that. *John's Gospel* also had this simple, absolutely central issue as its point: see John 20:31.

John uses three terms to describe God and the life of God that Christians share through Christ: *light, life,* and *love.* These are the three things everyone needs and wants more than anything else in the world. Their opposites, falsehood, death and hate, are the three worst things in the world. Everyone wants to avoid them and attain their opposites, but not everyone knows how. Jesus is the answer to that question—the most important question in the world.

SECOND JOHN: GOD'S COMMAND IS TO LOVE

This short letter is addressed to "the elect lady and to her children." This "lady" probably refers not to an individual but to a local church. Mother Church is a lady. The letter was written by John "the Elder" (v. 1) in his old age, probably about A.D. 90.

The basic theme is no new command but the command we had from the beginning (v. 5), the same theme we find in *John's Gospel* and his first letter: the primacy of love. Love is not a new but a very old idea, as old as God.

"Love" means for John not first of all a feeling but a life, that we must live in obedience to God's commands (v. 6). But God's command *is* to love. "The command, as you have heard from the beginning, is that you must all live in love" (v. 6). Therefore, love and obedience, love and God's commandment, love and law, are one.

Love is also discerning, not naive. It needs sound doctrine. Love needs truth. John, therefore, writes against the same false teaching he warned against in his previous writing, the denial of the incarnation of Christ (v. 7). It is false charity to love falsehood. As St. Thomas Aquinas says, "The greatest charity one can do to another is to lead him to the truth."

THIRD JOHN: IMITATE GOOD

This little letter is the shortest book of the Bible. It is a personal note in response to a situation that had come up in the churches in Asia Minor. John had sent out teachers who traveled from one local church to another with his apostolic authority. One local church leader, Gaius, had accepted them with Christian hospitality and generosity, while another, Diotrephes, had treated them arrogantly and selfishly, denying John's authority as an apostle. He had even driven out those Christians who had accepted the teachers sent by John (v. 10).

John writes this letter to praise and thank Gaius for "living in the truth" (v. 3) and to warn against Diotrephes, who tells "lies" (v. 10). The simple message of this letter is one of the main themes of John's other writings: the real difference between good and evil, light and darkness, truth and falsehood; the simple message, "Do not imitate evil, but imitate good," for "he who does good is of God" (v. 11).

TWENTY-FOUR

Warning against False Teaching: Jude

J UDE WAS THE "the brother of James" (v. 1), who was Jesus' "brother," that is, his cousin (Mk 6:3; Mt 13:55). This makes Jude one of Jesus' relatives too. These relatives did not believe in Jesus until after he rose from the dead (Jn 7:1-9; Acts 1:1-14), but they then became leaders in the early Church at Jerusalem (Acts 15:13-21).

There is such a strong similarity between *Jude* 4-18 and *2 Peter* 2:1-3:4 that one of these authors was probably quoting the other.

Jude's primary theme is false teaching. Most of the letters in the New Testament deal with this theme, but all of *Jude* is concerned with it. The language he uses is very strong. But as we have noted before, it is not cruel but kind to utter loud warnings when there is real danger and to tell the truth when falsehoods are rampant.

The false teachers Jude opposed taught both false doctrine and false ethics, false practice—two things that *always* go together. These teachers taught that since God was gracious (v. 4), they could live as they pleased. (Sound familiar?) Jude describes their character in a series of five stunning images from nature in verses 12 and 13. Jude reminds them of the aspect of God they forgot: justice and judgment. He recounts past acts of God's judgment on disobedient Israel, disobedient angels, and disobedient Sodom and Gomorrah.

Jude encourages his audience to "build yourselves up on your most holy faith" (v. 20), to stay in spiritual shape, on guard against error, but to "convince some, who doubt" (v. 22). He closes with a great doxology (closing word of praise and glory) in verses 24 and 25. In this little letter as throughout the Bible, the negative is real but the positive outweighs it.

TWENTY-FIVE

The Most Difficult Book in the Bible: An Introduction to Revelation

T HE *BOOK OF REVELATION*, or *Apocalypse*, the only prophetic book in the New Testament, is surely the strangest and hardest to interpret of all the books of the Bible.

Its style is neither the simple, sober, eyewitness description that we find in the Gospels and *Acts* (and in most of the historical books of the Old Testament), nor the straightforward principles and advice that we find in the epistles (and in most of the wisdom books in the Old Testament). Its closest biblical equivalent is some of the visions of *Ezekiel* and *Daniel.*

It is a visionary, highly poetical, even mystical book. It seems to most ordinary Catholics a closed book, even a dangerous book. For it suggests to them images of wild-faced, white-robed, black-bearded fanatics with signs saying, "The end is nigh!" It's true that many "kooky" theologies and sects have used this book to justify their pet ideas. They usually interpret the rest of the Bible in light of their interpretation of this book rather than vice versa. This is backwards, of course, for we must interpret the more obscure by the less obscure, not vice versa.

The very strangeness and mystery of this book fascinates some (usually the more curious and poetical minds), while discouraging others (usually the more sober and practical). I don't think God expects all of us to resonate with each of the books of the Bible equally. That's one reason he provided many books, not just one. Not everyone has a poetical bent, especially today. (Look at the shamefully prosaic translation of the Bible that all Catholics have had to put up with at Mass for the last twenty years!) But there are always more poets than non-poets in the world, so there are always many minds that are fascinated by this book.

The author was evidently a poet (I refer to both the human author and the divine author); and it takes a poet to understand a poet. I think we can understand this book only when the poetic, intuitive, unconscious, imaginative part of our brain (the "right brain") is used, not only the clear, rational, conscious, controlled part (the "left brain"). *Revelation* is like a museum of abstract art, not representational or naturalistic art. It is like an Ingmar Bergman movie. Better yet, it is like a medieval illuminated manuscript. If you feel a kinship with medieval illustrations for this book, I think you are closer than most modern people to the mindset that produced it.

It claims to be a divinely-sent vision or dream, not a waking observation. It is not a clever, clear, controlled *allegory*, but is full of mysterious *symbols* with multiple layers of meaning. It is more imagistic than conceptual. That is probably the reason why no consistent, rational, theological explanation of it, however honest and well-intentioned, has yet gained universal acceptance. For the same reason that it is harder to specify and delimit the meaning of a painting than a novel, it is harder to be sure what we are supposed to get out of this book than the rest of the Bible. Most of the rest of the Bible is relatively clear. For thousands of years, ordinary people understood it quite well without theology courses or seminary training. Anyone who really wants to know can find what St. Paul most centrally cares about, or what the *Psalms* mean. But not so easily with this book.

ITS MAIN POINT

Yet its main overall point is clear from its title. Unfortunately, many modern editions of the Bible include titles added by modern editors, for the original books of the Bible did not have titles separate from the books themselves. The titles were the first words of each book. (For the books were not books with covers, but scrolls.)

The correct title is crucial because it tells us the main, central point of the whole book. If we miss that, then all the details will be misunderstood because their significance is relative to how they serve that main point.

The original title of this book is not simply "Revelation," and certainly not "The Revelation of St. John." Look it up (1:1). It is "The Revelation of Jesus Christ."

The center of this book—and the center of all world history—is Christ, the same Christ we know from the Gospels. No matter how different in style this book is from the Gospels, its main point is identical to theirs: its point is a person. The main point is not the end of the world, or even the cosmic battle between good and evil, or the millennium, or the great tribulation, or the Antichrist, but Christ himself.

The only difference between this book and the Gospels is that it presents Christ in his Second Coming. We see Christ in glory rather than in humiliation. The cosmic Christ reveals himself universally, not just to the Jews.

When Jesus ascended into Heaven, his disciples, gazing up into Heaven, saw two angels who announced to them the Second Coming: "Men of Galilee, why do you stand looking into heaven? This Jesus, who was taken up from you into heaven, will come in the same way as you saw him go into heaven" (Acts 1:11). *Revelation* fulfills the third part of our Christian faith about history, which we proclaim each Sunday: "Christ has died, Christ is risen, *Christ will come again.*"

The early Church was full of longing—anxious, joyful,

operative, expectant longing for Christ's return. Where we see a gray vagueness when we look into the future, they saw golden glory. Why have we lost this? I think it is largely because the doctrine of the Second Coming has been so abused by fringe groups, sects, and theological factions warring over secondary details like the millennium (the thousand-year reign of Christ described in ch. 20). These groups get caught up in questions like: do we live before it, during it, after it, or is it not historical at all? Especially in Protestant fundamentalism, "premillennialism," "postmillennialism," and "amillennialism" have been bitter battle cries.

But *abusus non tollit usus*—the abuse of a thing does not take away its proper use. We need the *Book of Revelation* even more than past ages did. For we need to recapture the historic hope it expresses. Even faith and love are not complete without hope.

ITS UNITY

At first this book seems to be two books, not one. The first three chapters feature seven letters to seven Christian churches (congregations) in Asia ("Asia Minor," modern Turkey): Ephesus, Smyrna, Pergamum, Thyatira, Sardis, Philadelphia, and Laodicea. These churches and cities were real, not visionary. The ruins of some of them can still be seen today. They had real, specific, local problems, just like the churches St. Paul wrote his epistles to; and the seven letters address these problems. They give each church a kind of report card. Though the language is formal and sometimes symbolic, the problems were real. Some were so specific and local that no one knows any more what they were: for example, the problem with the "Nicolaitans."

But then the book suddenly takes off like a rocket ship into the heavens. Visions explode like firecrackers in the mind. Tongues turn into swords. Thunders speak. Burning mountains fall into the sea. Angels blow trumpets. Stars with names like Wormwood fall from the sky. Four horsemen ride across the sky bringing terrible plagues. Giant locusts sting and torture people. The sea turns to blood. No one can unroll a scroll except the Lamb. A dragon battles an angel, a woman, and a Lamb. Angels, elders, and the four living creatures frolic and worship around a golden throne and a sea of crystal. Finally, a golden city majestically descends to earth from the sky. What in the world (or out of it) is going on here?

Revelation is not two books, how ever great the difference between the first three chapters and the last nineteen. The author wants to show the members of those seven local congregations (and us too) that their little local problems are part of a great cosmic battle that is being fought even now. The real story behind the world's headlines is the battle that will not cease until its consummation at the end of time. What we do in our parishes and homes contributes to what Christ is doing: preparing the Second Coming. *That* is the final meaning of our daily work. Setting up chairs for a parish committee meeting is a contribution, however small, to this greatest of all wars. Our lives are parts of a far greater scenario and significance than the unaided human eye can see, greater even than the unaided human mind can imagine.

ITS AUTHOR

If a single author can write in two styles as different as those of *Revelation* 1-3 and 4-19, there is no reason to think it is impossible that the same John who wrote the fourth Gospel wrote this book, how ever different the style of those two books. From the earliest Christian writings that mention this book, tradition has always ascribed it to John the Evangelist. Yet since the mid-1700s, a number of Scripture scholars have come to the conclusion that it must have been a different John, largely because the style, form, and vocabulary are so different from that of *John's Gospel* and epistles.

Perhaps they are right, but the bottom line is that no one knows for sure. Each side is suspicious of the other side's authority that is invoked. On the one hand, there is the reliability of tradition. On the other hand, there is the reliability of the current crop of scholars. Personally, I would put my money on the Church Fathers sooner than on the Church's new kids on the block until proven otherwise.

Even my gut literary instincts tell me it "smells" Johannine. For the traditional symbol for John is the eagle; and this book, *John's Gospel*, and *1 John* soar like an eagle. The same Spirit moves over the waters of both worlds, however different the waters and the weather. Also, *1 John* and *Revelation* share some distinctive themes, notably the Antichrist and the vision of a cosmic battle between good and evil, an all-encompassing spiritual war.

ITS PURPOSE

It is often asserted (for example, in short introductions to this book printed in Bibles) that it was written to comfort Christians who were being persecuted. This is probably not untrue, but it tends to leave two mistaken impressions: (1) that the purpose of the book is comfort rather than truth, and (2) that its relevance is limited to the second century. (It was probably written between A.D. 90 and 100.)

The book itself says it was written not because John got it into his head to spread around some good cheer to poor souls, but because Jesus Christ revealed himself to John and commanded John to write down the vision. What better reason did anyone ever have for writing any book? Why substitute a lesser reason for a greater one?

Unless the fundamental claim made by this book right at the beginning is simply false—that is, unless this book is fundamentally a fake—its primary author is Jesus Christ, just as its primary subject is Jesus Christ. It is a self-revelation, a theophany. Just as if we forget its primary subject matter we misunderstand its content, so if we forget its primary author we read it in the wrong spirit: the spirit of curiosity and scholarship rather than the spirit of wonder and worship. The most important key to reading this book is profound, interior silence.

Like the Bible as a whole, this book is a love letter from Almighty God to us. It can be helpful at times to peer intently through the spectacles of a scholar at the passages in a love letter; but it is certainly wrong to adopt that as your essential posture, instead of lying back and listening to your lover sing beautiful poetry to you.

When we read this book, let us remember that Jesus, not John, and certainly not some contemporary commentator (like me), is its primary interpreter. He is its primary author, and the author has the authority to interpret his own work. Authority, after all, means something like "author's rights."

In our next three chapters, we will explore the symbols in this book, the theme of the end of the world, and the triumph of Christ the King.

TWENTY-SIX

The Symbols in Revelation

M OST OF THE BIBLE CAN BE understood without paying explicit attention to the principles of symbolism and correct versus incorrect ways to interpret them (though there are a few crucially important passages like "This is my body" where different interpretations, symbolic versus literal, have divided Christendom). But we cannot understand the *Book of Revelation* without understanding symbolism. When symbolism appears in the other books of the Bible, it appears as a secondary note, or in a few chapters. If we fail to understand the symbolic passages, there is still a lot left that we can understand. Not so in this book. If we don't "get" the symbols, we don't "get" most of the book.

Therefore, in order to understand this book, we need to back up for a moment, take our eyes off the book, and review some basic principles of interpretation. This long way around will prove the shortest in the long run because it will block us from many dead ends, many misunderstandings.

A first and obvious question, and the one most often asked, is: how are we to know whether we are supposed to interpret any given passage in the Bible literally or symbolically?

There is an extremely simple and commonsensical answer to this question. If the writer claims he has perceived the events he narrates with his physical eyes, in the physical world, or that someone else has done so, then the passage is to be interpreted literally. But if the narrator or his sources do not claim that they or anyone else were eyewitnesses, then it might be possible to interpret the Scriptures symbolically. Symbols express what outer eyes do not see.

For instance, all the language describing God, in his own eternal and essential nature, whether in *Revelation* or in any other book, must be symbolic, not literal simply because no human being has seen God at any time (Jn 1:18), until he becomes incarnate in Christ. He has no body, so he cannot literally sit on a golden throne or have a "strong right hand" and a "mighty arm." These are *symbols* for his power.

Another example: the creation story in *Genesis* 1 and 2 cannot be a literal eyewitness account because there *were* no eyewitnesses before God made any creatures with eyes, that is, until the fifth or sixth day.

This criterion alone does not automatically settle the issue for all passages, for fiction as well as fact may be in the literary form of eyewitness descriptions. For instance, the *Book of Job* is probably fiction, but its events are visible, except for God appearing to Job at the end. (God appears to the "inner eye" but not to the outer.) There are borderline cases, like Noah and Jonah, which could go either way. But clearly the Jewish Exodus and the parting of the Red Sea in the Old Testament, and the appearances of the resurrected Christ in the New Testament, are meant literally, as historical facts. And clearly the flying horsemen and angelic trumpets of *Revelation* are not—though they may *symbolize* future historical facts that are visible and literal.

A given passage may invite both a literal and symbolic interpretation, on different levels. For instance, Moses really existed and was also a symbol of Christ. Christ's healing of the blind man really happened, yet it also symbolizes his healing of our spiritual blindness. For God can use real events to symbolize other things, while we can only use words.

A second principle of interpretation is even more basic and important. It is frequently violated, for example, when someone says something like this: "You can interpret the resurrection literally if you wish, but I don't believe in miracles, and therefore I interpret those passages according to my sincerely held beliefs."

This confuses *interpretation* with *belief*. Even great scholars are often guilty of this confusion. We must *never* interpret a book—any book—in light of our own beliefs! We must *interpret* the book in the light of its *author's* beliefs. Then we *evaluate* it according to our own beliefs.

Interpreting a book by your own beliefs is *eisegesis*, "reading into" the book what's already in your own mind. All good interpretation is *exegesis*, "reading out" of the book what's in the *author's* mind.

When a modernist interprets miracle stories as fables, he is reversing the roles of interpretation and belief. When a fundamentalist interprets symbols literally, he is doing the same thing. For example, the fundamentalist might interpret the "millennium," the thousand-year reign of Christ on earth (ch. 20), as a thousand literal, historical years. Or he might interpret the 144,000 saved as a literal number, as the Jehovah's Witnesses do. (Get your seats while the tickets last; Heaven's stadium isn't very big!)

The *Book of Revelation* claims to be a spiritual vision, not a material one, seen by the inner eye, not the outer one. It is a dream to John's mind by Sonlight, by Christ, not a sensation sent to his optic nerves by earthly sunlight.

A third principle needs to be added: interpreting a passage symbolically does not necessarily mean not interpreting it *historically*. For instance, the story of the Fall in *Genesis* 3 is clearly symbolic but historical. The tree, the fruit, and the serpent function in the story not as things in themselves but as symbols of evil, temptation, and Satan. For example, Satan is not literally a snake. Yet the story must be *historical* because its subject, sin, is a historical fact. The story tells us how sin originated. If sin and its origin are not historical facts, then salvation and *its* origin (Christ's death and resurrection) need not be historical facts either.

The events in *Revelation* are historical events. Some are past (for example, the birth of Christ and the flight into Egypt, Rv 12:1-6). Most are future. But all are told symbolically rather than literally (for example, compare Rv 12:1-6 with Mt 1:18-2:23).

Many people think that there are only two ways to interpret any passage: either literally and historically, or symbolically and non-historically, like Job or the Prodigal Son. But there is a third possibility: symbolic *and* historical, like *Revelation.*

A fourth principle: do not confuse symbolism with allegory. In allegory, each ingredient has one and only one fully definable correct meaning. In symbolism, there may be many correct meanings and they may or may not be exactly definable. For example, the Antichrist probably means both a single historical individual who will appear at the end of time, and also a spiritual force which was already in the world in the first century (see 1 Jn 2:18,22; 4:3). The symbol of thunder for God's voice, used frequently in *Revelation,* is not simply an allegory for power, or fear, or a voice from Heaven; it connotes more than it denotes. You must feel the awe, not just figure out the meaning, to understand such a rich symbol.

A fifth principle in interpreting scriptural symbolism is to compare Scripture with Scripture, to interpret Scripture by Scripture. For example, we interpret the Lamb in *Revelation* in light of John the Baptist's words about Jesus (Jn 1:29,36) and the liturgical offering in *Leviticus;* and vice versa. The sea out of which the beast comes (Rv 13:1) usually symbolizes death in Scripture (for example, Moses crossing the Red Sea, and Noah's flood). Thus, the fact that there is no sea in Heaven (Rv 21:1) is not a threat to surfers and sailors but a symbol for eternal life.

Where, specifically, do you go to find the correct interpretation of a symbol in Scripture, especially in this book, the most symbolic book in Scripture? I think we can divide its symbols into six groups by this standard.

1. Some symbols are explicitly explained in the same passage in which they are given. For example, just as Jesus interprets the parable of the sower to his disciples in *Matthew* 13, he explains the symbols of the seven stars and seven lampstands to John (1:20).

2. Some symbols are explained elsewhere in Scripture, for example, the Lamb and his blood, and the sea, as explained above.

3. Some are plain and obvious, for example, the angels (messengers) of the plagues, and the seals (secrets) of the book (God's plan) that no one but the Lamb (Christ) could open (fulfill) (5:1-9).

4. Some *suggest* to the reader a hidden meaning, for example, the number 666, the mark of the beast (Antichrist) (13:18). The text says, "This calls for wisdom." We are invited to solve the puzzle. The probable solution is that the letters of the blasphemous divine title that the Roman Emperor Domitian (A.D. 81-96) took for himself translate into the number 666 by using standard ancient number code (a=1, b=2, etc.) Domitian began the first virulent persecution of Christians while John was writing this book.

5. Some symbols are intuited with the instinctive poetic imagination, for example, the door in Heaven (4:1), the silence in Heaven (8:1), and the war in Heaven (12:7).

6. Finally, some are not clear from any of the above sources, for example, the two witnesses (11:3) and the number of the horsemen (9:16).

Put all the symbols together and ask what, most obviously and ubiquitously, do they all teach? The answer is: spiritual warfare. *Revelation* describes a cosmic battle between good and evil, light and darkness, Heaven and Hell, Christ and the Antichrist.

Every important good has a parallel evil symbol in *Revelation*. Parallel to the holy Trinity there is the unholy trinity of the dragon (Satan), the beast (Antichrist), and his false prophet (for the Holy Spirit is the Spirit of the true prophets). Parallel to the holy city of Jerusalem, the city of God, there is the unholy city of Babylon, the city of the world. (These two symbols were the basis of St. Augustine's *The City of God*, the all-time classic Christian philosophy of history.) Parallel to the Blessed Virgin Mary (who also symbolizes the Church) is the "whore of Babylon." Parallel to the sea of crystal, there is the lake of fire.

The point is that evil is only an imitation of good, a parasite on good. Nothing is evil in the beginning. Evil cannot win; it is dependent on good. It can do enormous, horrible harm, but it cannot win in the end. If the parasite succeeded in destroying all the good in its host, it would destroy itself as well.

The parasitic nature of evil is shown even in the number symbolism. The number for evil is either three sixes (the number of the Antichrist), or three-and-one-half ("a time, times, and half a time"—12:14). Now seven is the sacred number. There are seven churches, seven angels, seven stars, seven candlesticks. Six is a defective seven, and three-and-one-half is a broken seven.

Twelve is also a sacred number, but an earthly, not a heavenly one. We immediately think of the twelve tribes of Israel and twelve apostles as the pillars of the Church, the New Israel, the New Jerusalem (21:10-21). The number 144,000 —the number of the elect, the saints, the saved (7:4; 14:1)— is twelve (tribes) times twelve (apostles) times one thousand. To the ancients, "a thousand" signified an unimaginably and indefinitely vast multitude.

Probably the most common mistake in interpreting the symbolism in *Revelation* is to attempt a strict chronology of events, to try to use it to figure out when the end of the world will come. This is a mistake for five reasons. First, the events are not in chronological sequence. Any attempt to interpret them sequentially meets insuperable contradictions. Second, the numbers in *Revelation* are symbolic, not literal. Third, Christ himself said he did not know when the end of the world would come (Mt 24:36). How incredibly arrogant to claim to know more than your Lord! Fourth, every single predictor of the end of the world so far has been wrong. How reasonable is it to put any confidence in whatever batter is now at the plate if every batter who has ever tried to get a hit off *this puzzling pitcher* has struck out? Fifth, and most important of all, it is the wrong focus; it is misunderstanding the central point of the book to seek a strict chronology that points to the end of the world. The point of this book is not *when* but *who*. Its focus is on the One who comes, the Christ. In this, it continues and consummates the central focus of the entire Bible.

TWENTY-SEVEN

Christ the King in Revelation

A S WE HAVE SEEN, anyone who reads *Revelation* primarily to forecast or describe the end of the world is missing its central point, indeed, the central point of history. This point of all things is not a *when* or a *how* but a *who*. At the center of this book, at the center of the whole Bible, at the center of all history, stands Jesus Christ.

We find Christ on every page of *Revelation*. *Revelation* is no less Christocentric than the Gospels. The only difference is that here he wears not a cross but a crown.

The book is a series of visions. The first, controlling vision (ch. 1) is the vision of the "son of man" (v. 13) who is "the first and the last, and the living one; I died, and behold, I am alive forevermore, and I have the keys to Death and Hades" (vv. 17-18). This is Christ the King of the universe: of Heaven, earth, and even the underworld, for he has been in all three worlds (see 1 Pt 3:18-22).

The one who sends the seven letters to the seven churches (ch.s 2 and 3) is none other than Christ, as is clear from the last words of each of the seven letters.

The one seated on the heavenly throne (4:2), surrounded by twenty-four elders in white garments and golden crowns, by lightning, thunder, fire, and the sea of crystal (4:2-6), is Christ. The vision of Isaiah 6:1-5 is repeated here (4:8-9), and now finally interpreted and identified as a vision of Christ.

The one, the only one, who can open the scroll and its seven seals (5:5) is Christ. The scroll is history, his-story. The scroll is also our story, our destiny, and our salvation. He alone can fulfill both stories. The one who receives "power and wealth and wisdom and might and honor and glory and blessing" is "the Lamb who was slain" (5:12). The whole story of human history (the scroll) is about him. He is the hidden key to history. (See G.K. Chesterton's classic *The Everlasting Man* for a brilliant book-length proof of that statement.) The vision of the "great multitude which no man could number... standing before the throne and before the Lamb" (7:9) is again Christ, this time in his Mystical Body, his Church, his people.

History ends in chapter 8. "When the Lamb opened the seventh seal, there was silence in heaven for half an hour" (8:1)—so awful is the sight. The seven angelic trumpets that follow, like the seven seals, are the ending to his story.

Finally, "the seventh angel blew his trumpet, and there were loud voices in Heaven saying, 'The kingdom of this world has become the kingdom of our Lord and of his Christ, and he shall reign for ever and ever'" (11:15). History ends with the Hallelujah Chorus!

The next chapter begins with a flashback vision of Christ and his mother, the "woman clothed with the sun" (12:1), and continues with a "war in Heaven" between St. Michael the archangel and Satan, the "accuser of our brethren" (12:10), who "have conquered him *by the blood of the Lamb*" (12:11, emphasis mine). Again, we find the Gospel, the same Gospel and the same Christ, but in symbol rather than in incarnate human flesh, and in glory rather than in suffering.

Christ's defeat of Satan is continued in chapter 13, and chapter 14 begins with another Christ-vision: "... on Mount Zion stood the Lamb, and with him a hundred and forty-four thousand who had his name..." (v. 1). They "sing a new song"—the Gospel. "No one could learn that song except the hundred and forty-four thousand who had been redeemed..." (14:3). One hundred and forty-four thousand equals twelve (tribes of Israel) times twelve (apostles) times one thousand (the multitude of converted pagans).

There is also a song in chapter 15, "the song of Moses" (v. 3; compare with Ex 15). But this song is now called "the song of the Lamb" (15:3), thus identifying Moses as a Christ-figure and Judaism as proto-Christianity.

Three chapters of "the wrath of God" (16:1) follow, under the image of the seven bowls poured out by the angels (messengers) of God. Even this is Christocentric, for his judgment is only the inescapable alternative to his salvation. As the light necessarily makes its own darkness around it, the Savior necessarily makes his own shadow of damnation as the alternative to salvation for those who refuse him.

After chapter 18's moving and massive mourning for the fall of Babylon (Babel), the great city of the world, chapter 19 contains the triumph song of the winner in the last, greatest, and—in reality—*only* war of all time (see Eph 6:12). This is also Christocentric, for its "hallelujah" celebrates his marriage to the Church, his Bride (19:7).

The latter half of chapter 19 presents Christ again, this time with four names. Three are already known from Scripture: "Faithful and True" (v. 11), "The Word of God" (v. 13), and "King of kings and Lord of lords" (v. 16). But he also "has a name inscribed which no one knows but himself" (v. 12). There is more, infinitely more, to Christ than we can know. We will learn this new name (identity, dimension) only in Heaven.

We too will have a new name in Heaven, described in the same words: "... I will give him a white stone with a new name written on the stone which no one knows except him who receives it" (2:17). Your ultimate identity is a secret known only to you and God.

In a sense the whole *Book of Revelation* is about Christ's new name. It tells more about Christ than the Gospels tell, but more about the same Christ: glory added to suffering, crown added to cross, Second Coming added to first coming, return added to ascension (see Acts 1:11).

The "millennium" (ch. 20), about which so much controversy has swirled in certain Christian circles (between the premillennialists, postmillennialists, and amillennialists), is presented as a thousand-year reign *of Christ* (20:4). Losing the focus on Christ for a focus on time was the first cause of the theological bickering.

Chapter 21 describes the last event in history: the coming of the Church, the New Jerusalem, Christ's Mystical Body, in all its glory descending from Heaven. "And I saw the holy city, new Jerusalem, coming down out of heaven from God, prepared as a bride adorned for her husband..." (21:2). Just as God's call "down" to Abraham (Gn 12) comes right after the fall of the "uppity" Tower of Babel (Gn 11), so the descent of the New Jerusalem (ch. 21) comes after the fall of proud Babylon, the continuation of Babel in chapter 18.

This Bride, by the way, is not many cities or many brides but one—not churches but the Church. Christ is no bigamist. When he comes, he will not marry a harem but a bride.

Christ the King is our King *so that* he can be our Bridegroom. The deepest thing is not power but love. Power is only a means to love. Christ exercises his power so that he can consummate his love.

The final cause, end, purpose, goal, ultimate good, meaning of life, point, and conclusion of the whole story that began with the "Big Bang" (Gn 1:1)—providentially steered through every stellar explosion and terrestrial evolution, every molecule and every meeting, every hair's and sparrow's fall—is Christ's marriage to his Church.

The world exists for the Church. The universe exists for the Church, as the raw material the Church is made from. Gases and galaxies are not its point, only its wires and wheels.

God went to all the trouble of creation, incarnation, death, resurrection, ascension, and this final consummation of history for his marriage to the Church.

Some find *Revelation* hard, dry, threatening, repellent, cruel, impersonal, and unemotional. But if we belong to Christ, we should read it with a lump in our throat and a leap in our heart, for we are his bride. *Revelation* culminates in our wedding night.

The only ones who should find this book threatening are the wicked, who call on the mountains and rocks to fall on them and hide them from the face of God, which they fear (6:16). To fear the face of God, which is truth, is, quite simply, to be bound for Hell. To love the face of God is to be bound for Heaven.

Perhaps Heaven and Hell are the same place, or made of the same substance, the same substance everything is made of, namely truth, the one thing that is inescapable. To love it and live on it as our food, is Heaven. To hate and fear it and to be tortured by it, is Hell. For truth is inescapable; God can no more turn off the light of his truth than the sun can stop shining.

The book ends (ch. 22) with the invitation to join the wedding feast, that is, the good news (*evangelium*) sent by Christ through his *angelium* or angel (v. 16). This news is the free offer of salvation (v. 17).

"The Spirit and the Bride (Church) say, 'Come.'" Both God and the visible Church have as their primary work on earth the invitation to come to Christ's wedding feast. "And let him who hears say, 'Come.'" The Christian responds, "Come, Lord Jesus!" (22:20). Without this passionate longing for our love feast, our Christian faith is deeply impaired and incomplete. "And let him who is thirsty come. Let him who desires take the water of life [salvation] without price." Our only qualification is thirst, desire. All who seek, find (Mt 7:7).

The one thing we can be absolutely certain of is that we will die. If you were to die tonight and stand before God, and he were to ask you, "Why should I take you to Heaven?" What would you say?

We can argue forever about your answer or my answer, but here is God's answer. It is on almost every page of the New Testament: because of Christ, the water of eternal life is free, "without price." All we have to do is to believe in it, in him; hope in it, in him; love it, love him. Not worthiness but love and desire is our only qualification. Heaven, like the Church, is not a museum for saints but a hospital for sinners. We are bums who have been given clean wedding garments (Mt 22:12) and free entrance tickets to the wedding. The real surprise is: we are not guests at all, we're the Bride.

TWENTY-EIGHT

The Second Coming in Revelation

S OME TIME DURING THE FIRST HALF of this century—the Christian half, for the event recounted here could never have happened in *this* half—a question was asked of major American newspaper editors: What would be the greatest headline you could ever hope to write? Many chose something like: *All Wars End* or *Cure for Cancer.* But a Chicago editor gave the best answer: *Christ Comes Again.*

Of course, when he does come again, we won't be bothering about things like newspapers. Only God will write history's greatest headline.

Revelation is, as Paul Harvey would say, "The rest of the story." It is about the last act of our play, the end of history, of time itself. More specifically, it is about Christ's Second Coming. The specific theme determines the general theme, not vice versa. Christ does not come again *because* it is the end of time. It is the end of time *because* he comes again. Christ is not relative to time; time is relative to Christ.

Revelation, like the rest of the Bible, is Christocentric. Christ's coming again is not so much the *Second Coming* of Christ as the *full reign of Christ.* Revelation is the completion of the Gospel.

Many readers and interpreters of *Revelation* are more interested in the *when* than in the *who*. But the only answer he gives to the *when* question is "soon," or "quickly" (3:11; 22:7, 12, 20).

But it's been nearly two thousand years already. That hardly seems "soon." Did he lie?

Not at all. For "the Lord is not slow about his promise as some count slowness, but is forbearing toward you, not wishing that any should perish, but that all should reach repentance" (2 Pt 3:9). How dare we complain about being given extra time before final exams?

Furthermore, God's time is not like ours. "For a thousand years in thy sight are but as yesterday when it is past, or as a watch in the night" (Ps 90:4).

When will you die? "Soon." Whether in sixty minutes or sixty years, death is always soon. Life is always short. Similarly, when will time die? When will the whole world's life end? Soon.

Real time is measured not by clocks but by meanings, not by matter moving across space but by spirit moving across purposes. Real time is qualitative, not quantitative; personal, not impersonal. The Greek language has two different words for these two different kinds of time: *kairos* for the first (real, lived time) and *kronos* for the second (clock time).

All the time between Christ's first and second comings is minor in meaning, relatively insignificant, compared to these two great events. The fall of Rome, the rise and fall of the Middle Ages, the Renaissance, the industrial revolution, two world wars—these are mere footnotes in God's history book, page two items in God's newspapers. *Revelation* tells us the headlines.

"When will Grandma come back from Florida?" asks the breathlessly expectant three-year-old. "Soon." Now all the time until Grandma comes will be defined by that event, and it will indeed be "soon," not because it is a certain quantity of clock time but because Grandma is such an important person in the toddler's life.

And Christ's Second Coming is infinitely more than Grandma's. It is the consummation of our divine spouse's engagement to his Bride, his Church. It is God coming to marry us. If it takes ten thousand years, it will be "soon."

Expectation of a happy thing before it happens adds to its happiness. Planning a movie, a ball game, or a vacation is part of the fun. But this is infinitely more than a vacation. This is eternal marriage to God. Therefore, this book should make every Christian very, very happy.

For the thing we hope for above all else is here promised, assured, guaranteed. The great King will come to defeat all his enemies and take us, his Cinderella, to his great castle to live happily ever after. The fairy tales are foolish not because they are too good to be true, but because they are not nearly good enough. "What no eye has seen, nor ear heard, nor the heart of man conceived, what God has prepared for those who love him" (1 Cor 2:9).

But we would still like to know just how soon that will be. Might he come in our own lifetime? Indeed he might. Might it be that the apparent clues in this century are his first footfalls? Yes, it might be. Israel's return to her homeland in 1948, after 1,878 years, is often seen as an apocalyptic sign. Another sign might be the first faint, tentative talk of rebuilding the Temple, reported by *Time* magazine. A third seems to be the appearances of Our Lady at Lourdes and Fatima and now, possibly, at Medjugorje with apocalyptic-sounding messages. (But the really startling sign of the end would be a World Series between the Red Sox and the Cubs.)

I have heard some fundamentalists predicting the world will end in 1996 because: (1) the world was created in 4004 B.C. according to Ussher's literal calculation from the Old Testament genealogies, (2) Christ was born in 4 B.C. (our calendar is off four years), and (3) 1996 would bring us to six "days" since a thousand years are as one day and one day are as a thousand years to God (2 Pt 3:8). Thus 1996 would begin the seventh "day" of eternal Sabbath rest.

This calculation (fairly typical of many others) is probably fallacious for three reasons. First, the genealogies cannot be calculated literally without contradictions. Second, no reputable scientist in the world thinks the earth is only six thousand years old. Third, and most importantly, Jesus himself said he did not know when the world would end (Mt 24:36, 42-44; Lk 17:20-24). How presumptuous of a Christian to outguess Christ! Furthermore, as we've already seen, every single prediction has been false so far. Their collective batting average is .000; why trust the ones who are up at the plate now?

God tells us in Scripture quite clearly not only *that* we do not know the date but also *why:* so that we would be ready at any and every time (Mt 24:42-44). If we knew it would be even as "soon" as 1996, we would probably procrastinate until 1995. Then suddenly we would "get religion," thus wasting the time before 1995. It may well be tonight!

The end of time and the beginning of eternity, the end of the world and the beginning of Heaven, are symbolized in *Revelation* by the fall of Babylon, the city of the world (ch. 18) and the descent of the new Jerusalem, the City of God (ch. 21).

What a strange and wonderful juxtaposition of images to end the story of all stories! The first one symbolizes the fall of worldly power, of the Tower of Babel, of Babylon, the captors and enemies of God's chosen people, of Rome, of civilization, and of human pride. (For a single symbol can mean all these things and many more.) The second image is even more striking: in the place of this worldly city springing up, there majestically descends from Heaven a great golden city, God's masterpiece, the Church, in all her bridal purity and beauty. This is the consummation of the kingdom of God. This is the city of which Jerusalem was only a symbol.

It is the perfect finish to the story of clashing symbols that we find throughout Scripture. There is perfect consistency to all the vertical images: all human ways up to God fail, all divine ways down to man succeed. Chapters 18 and 21 of *Revelation* only complete this consistent pattern.

First, we see God reaching down to create a world that is

perfectly good. Then we see a human hand reaching up to snatch the forbidden fruit, and this apparent rise is really the fall.

Next, the Tower of Babel (Gn 11) seems perfectly reasonable and destined for success, but the attempt to reach Heaven by human effort collapses. Then comes the call of Abraham, in the very next chapter. It seems like a perfectly ridiculous way to save history, yet it is God's beginning to the world's greatest success story, the story of redemption.

Later, Job's (Everyman's) attempts to find God seem perfectly right and just, yet they do not succeed. But when God finds Job, even impatient Job is satisfied.

All the false prophets seem to succeed. They are popular, for they measure God by what their hearers want. True prophets, on the other hand, are always unpopular and persecuted since they measure humanity by God, not God by humanity. Yet they alone know the truth and survive through the ages.

All human expectations of the Messiah are wrong. He corresponds to none of the ideas our minds conjure up: earthly king, warrior, politician, philosopher, Levitical priest, or even merely a prophet. But God's idea is the most brilliant strategy ever conceived. He defeats the devil and redeems us by becoming a crucified criminal. By his death he reconciles earth and Heaven, justice and mercy, at once on the cross (Ps 85:10).

Finally, at the end, Babylon—all worldly grasping and glory —collapses in one hour. The despair is stunning. Please read the great poetry of chapter 18, not just these thin words about it. After the false ladder from earth to Heaven collapses, the true ladder from Heaven to earth appears: the New Jerusalem is Christ himself, the Head and his Body, the Church. (He is revealed as the real Jacob's ladder in Jn 1:29-34.)

Revelation preaches the same Gospel in symbols that Jesus preached in deeds and Paul in words: salvation by God's grace, not man's greatness. Other religions are stories of man's search for God. The Bible is the story of God's search for man. Jesus promised us that all who seek him will find him (Lk 11:9-13), but that is only because he has first sought and found us. And this divine search-and-rescue operation, which theologians call redemption, is completed only when history itself is completed, when our divine lover comes to fetch his bride to take her home.

Afterword

WHAT NOW? What next?

Don't read this book again. Read the New Testament again. And again. And again. Pray it again. And again. And again.

Reading a book like this one—a book about a book—can be useful, but it also can be dangerous. It can substitute a second thing for a first thing, like preferring a picture of a person to a person. The New Testament itself is only a picture of a person. This book is only a beginner's tour guide to the picture. What matters—the *only* thing that matters, in the end—is persons, and their relationship to this divine Person whose picture this book is.

Christ caught the Pharisees with their nose in the Old Testament, refusing to look up at him and come to him, even though that book's whole purpose was to lead them to him (Jn 5:39). They forgot that a book is a sign, *not reality in itself.* It points beyond itself. It's like a window: we're meant to look *through* it, not *at* it. The Bible is such a precious window because of the one whom we see through it. It is a more precious window than the window in a prison cell that is the prisoner's only light. We are all prisoners of sin, and this book is our window to Christ our only Light.

More than a window, it is a door. We must walk through it, not just look through it. We must do it, not just read and pray about it (see Mt 7:24-27). And do it again.

Both as a window and a door, the New Testament is inexhaustible. There is no end of the light that comes through it, and no end of the transactions between Heaven and earth that can be carried on by praying it. It thus teaches us to see all the world and all of life as windows and doors, as transparent things, not opaque things, as channels and conduits between God and us. The whole world is between. God can't be placed relative to the world—in it or out of it—but the world is placed relative to God, as the very relation between God and us, God's other book. If we learn the habit of seeing everything in the world as the between instead of as an opaque, final thing—if we learn to read and pray the whole world as we read and pray the Bible, as God's book, God's Word, God's love letter—then we are well on the way to becoming wise, which means simply living in reality.

Your Guide to Reading the Old Testament

You Can Understand the Old Testament
A Book-by-Book Guide for Catholics
Peter Kreeft

For lay Catholics who are intimidated or overwhelmed by the sheer size and complexity of the Old Testament, Peter Kreeft offers a clear road map. With keen insight and engaging wit, he focuses on the core message of each book and its relevance for today, transforming dry study into spiritually satisfying adventures in God's Word.

Discover how God begins his "rescue operation" after the fall of Adam and Eve in the Garden of Eden. Meet Isaiah, "the Shakespeare of Prophecy," and listen to his prophecies "thunder with the message of salvation." Or witness "the sweet of history" in Daniel's prophecies about the fall of might empires and ages to come. *You Can Understand the Old Testament* will take you on a fascinating and rewarding tour that probes the spiritual meaning of Scripture. *$8.99*